P9-CEV-746

The Irish Spirit

The Irish Spirit

Recipes Inspired by the Legendary Drinks of Ireland

by Margaret M. Johnson

Photographs by Leigh Beisch and Margaret M. Johnson

CHRONICLE BOOKS

SAN FRANCISCO

For friends near and far, and the Irish spirit in all of us.
Sláinte!

Text copyright © 2006 by Margaret M. Johnson.
Plated food photographs copyright © 2006 by Leigh Beisch.
Scenic photographs copyright © 2006 by Margaret M. Johnson.

All rights reserved. No part of this book may be reproduced in any form
without written permission from the publisher.

Library of Congress Cataloging-in-Publication Data available.

ISBN-10: 0-8118-5042-0
ISBN-13: 978-0-8118-5042-1

Manufactured in China.

Designed and typeset by Tim Belonax
Photography Assistance: Angelica Cao
Food Stylist: George Dolese
Food Stylist Assistant: Elisabet Der Nederlanden
Prop Stylist: Sara Slavin

Distributed in Canada by Raincoast Books
9050 Shaughnessy Street
Vancouver, British Columbia V6P 6E5

10 9 8 7 6 5 4 3 2

Chronicle Books LLC
680 Second Street
San Francisco, California 94107

www.chroniclebooks.com

The photographs listed are used with courtesy of the following.
Pages 2, 6, 10 (bottom), 79, 102 (bottom), 105: Irish Distillers; page 46
(bottom): Diages/Guinness; page 76 (bottom): Tourism Ireland; and page
102 (top): Shannon Development.

ACKNOWLEDGMENTS

I'd like to express my thanks to the countless chefs, chef-proprietors, and Irish product manufacturers who originally contributed recipes for this book. I would also like to acknowledge the cooperation and support of the Irish brewers and distillers who provided history, lore, and products: Biddy Early Brewery; Boisset America; Bunratty Mead & Liqueur Company; Carlow Brewing Company; Castle Brands; Cider Industry Council; Cochrane and Cantrell; John Teeling, Managing Director, Cooley Distillery; Diageo/Guinness; Heineken Murphy Brewery; Hilden Brewery; Hot Irishman; Kinsale Brewery; Knockeen Hills Irish Poteen; Pernod Ricard/Irish Distillers; and Saint Brendan's Irish Cream. Thanks also to Bord Bia (Irish Food Board) in Dublin and Chicago; Orla Carey of Tourism Ireland; Roisin Hennerty and Molly O'Loughlin of the Irish Dairy Board, Chicago; Madeleine Morel, my agent, who continues to provide guidance and encouragement; Bill LeBlond, senior editor, Chronicle Books, for his faith in me again; and Amy Treadwell, for her editorial assistance. Finally, heartfelt thanks to my husband, Carl, for his continued indulgence in all things Irish!

PERMISSIONS

The recipe for Bushmills Duck au Poivre (page 18) is used with the permission of Bushmills; the recipe for Hot Irishman Meringues (page 34) is used with permission of Bernard Walsh, Managing Director of Hot Irishman; "The Legend of Biddy Early" (page 66) is used with permission of Niall Garvey, managing director of Biddy Early Brewery; the recipes for Tomato-Basil Soup (page 80), Apple Cake with Toffee Sauce (page 96), and Fruity Sponge Cake with Cider Sabayon (page 101) are used with permission of the Cider Industry Council; "Mead: The Wedding Story" (page 123) is used with permission of Nancy Larkin, the Bunratty Winery; the recipe for Carolans Strawberry and Meringue Crunch (page 136) is used with permission of Cochrane and Cantrell; the recipe for Baileys Chocolate Pots (page 138) is used with permission of Bord Bia (Irish Food Board); the recipe for Baileys White Chocolate Tart with Raspberry Coulis (page 144) is used with the permission of Diageo/R&A Bailey; the recipe for Saint Brendan's Oatmeal–Chocolate Mint Cookies (page 147) is used with permission of Ciaran Mulgrew, managing director of Saint Brendan's Irish Cream Liqueur Co. Ltd.

TABLE OF CONTENTS

INTRODUCTION

In his praise of grape and grain, the late wine aficionado Alec Waugh once suggested that "man has been accorded by a kindly nature four stout companions to sustain and console him on his terrestrial pilgrimage: wine, spirits, fortified wines, and beer." These drinks, he said, "provide solace, relaxation, and stimulus that a man needs if he is to complete with equanimity his arduous and often arid journey."

For centuries, the marriage of wine with food has been an equally happy one. Chefs, food writers, and wine critics continue to extol the perfect partnership they create and the way that ordinary recipes are elevated to extraordinary dishes with a mere splash of red or a dash of white. The late Alexis Lichine, wine grower and author of the landmark *Encyclopedia of Wines and Spirits*, called the use of wine in cooking "a positive pleasure [in which] the two combine in a gastronomic treat infinitely more delicious than either could provide alone."

As most cooks know, wine is not used in cooking for its alcoholic content, but as a seasoning that enhances the natural flavors of foods with a mere suggestion of its presence. Through the years, imaginative cooks have learned to baste, marinate, tenderize, flambé, sauté, and deglaze with wine, in recipes ranging from crêpes and chops and seafood to soups.

But this book is not about wine—although James Joyce called Guinness "the wine of Ireland" and Czar Peter the Great endorsed Irish whiskey with the acclamation "of all wines, the Irish spirit is the best." It is, instead, an attempt to form new alliances, create new marriages, and use the best of Ireland's legendary drinks in exciting and delicious recipes.

The idea of a cookbook based on such relationships seems to be a logical extension of Waugh's philosophy, as well as of my own strange notions concerning Irish food and drink. Let's face it, Ireland hasn't typically been known for its cuisine. For boiled potatoes and Irish stew, yes, but not for a cuisine in the same way we view French or Italian food. On the other hand, Ireland has almost always been associated with its national institution—the pub—and visitors there extol the pleasures of "sharing a jar," "pulling a pint," or getting into the Irish spirit! With an estimated 11,000 pubs in the Republic of Ireland, 1,650 in Northern Ireland, and more than 1,000 in Dublin alone, it's no wonder that visitors frequently number among their fondest memories the pubs they've visited. Indeed, the Irish pub is the center of Irish life, and it's the place where an estimated 2 million pints of stout are consumed daily!

By now, however, savvy travelers to Ireland have experienced the culinary revolution that's been evolving over the past few decades. Irish chefs have been steadily taking advantage of the country's natural bounty of produce, meat, and fish to develop a national food identity. What better way to accomplish this than to combine the pleasures of the pub with some creativity in the kitchen?

History tells us that in the absence of a wine-growing tradition, beer becomes a nation's favorite drink. And like wine, which chefs have long known enhances the taste and flavor of food, Ireland's beer and ale, along with its whiskey, cider, and mead, have been natural partners in many dishes, from plumping up the fruit in a Christmas pudding to tenderizing the meat in a casserole or pie. With the addition of Irish cream liqueurs, whiskey-based liqueurs, and spirit-flavored mustard, honey, and marmalade, there seems to be no end to the ways in which Ireland's legendary drinks are creating culinary partnerships to complement centuries-old traditions. They are, in fact, providing a new way to look at Irish cooking.

In *The Irish Spirit*, a revised edition of *Cooking with Irish Spirits*, you'll discover exciting ways to use Irish whiskey in dishes ranging from chicken liver pâté to marmalade puddings, and you'll see how whiskey-based liqueurs like Irish Mist and Celtic Crossing add just the right touch of sweetness to lamb and pork dishes. You'll learn how to glaze a ham or scallops in Irish cider, braise lamb shanks in Guinness stout, and mix Bunratty Mead into vinaigrette to toss with a salad. And if you thought Irish cream liqueurs like Baileys and Carolans were best for after-dinner drinks, you'll delight at using them in desserts such as cheesecakes, trifles, and chocolate pots.

You'll find that the "wines of Ireland" that once held provenance in the pub are finding a new place in the kitchen, lending themselves to creations infinitely more delicious than anyone could have imagined. I hope you'll enjoy serving some of the recipes offered in *The Irish Spirit*, a cookbook devoted exclusively to the marriage of food and wine, Irish-style.

Sláinte and *bon appétit!*

CHAPTER ONE

Whiskey with an "E"

Most historians agree that missionary monks around the sixth century brought the secret of distillation to Ireland, probably from the Middle East. They discovered that the alembic the Arabs used for distilling perfume could be put to better use, and they learned to make it in a pot still. They found that if a mash of barley and water was fermented with yeast and then heated in a pot still, the alcohol in it could be separated and retained, yielding a spirit with wondrous powers. They called it *uisce beatha* (pronounced isk'ke ba'ha), Irish for "water of life."

When the soldiers of Henry II first visited Ireland in the twelfth century, they were greatly impressed with this liquid. They had difficulty pronouncing it, however, and eventually *uisce* was anglicized, first to *fuisce*, and finally to the word "whiskey" we know today. The original official grant to distill whiskey in Ireland was issued in 1609 at Old Bushmills, in County Antrim, but the distilling tradition on that site stretches back to as early as 1276.

For centuries, the fashion for Irish whiskey was widespread. Queen Elizabeth I was said to be very partial to it, almost certainly acquiring the taste from Sir Walter Raleigh, who, by his own records, stopped off in County Cork on his way to Guyana to receive "a supreme present of a 32-gallon cask of the Earl of Cork's home-distilled *uisce beatha.*"

In 1750, Dr. Samuel Johnson defined it in glowing terms in his new dictionary: "Uisce Beatha (an Irish and Erse word that signifies the 'Water of Life') is a compounded distilled spirit, being drawn on aromaticks; and the Irish sort is particularly distinguished for its pleasant and mild flavour. The Highland sort is somewhat hotter, and by corruption in Scottish, they call it Whisky."

Indeed, the difference between Scotch whisky, "the highland sort," and Irish whiskey is far greater than the spelling. Irish whiskey is made from water, unmalted barley, and malted barley (the malting occurs when the barley is spread out on a warm floor and allowed to sprout or germinate before being dried). But unlike Scotch whisky, the barley used for Irish whiskey is dried with hot air in closed kilns rather than over an open peat fire. This ensures a honeyed rather than a smoky taste, making it a delicious ingredient in cooking as well as a fine drink. A triple distillation rather than a double one (as in Scotch whisky) in giant copper pot stills ensures the maximum purity of Irish whiskey, which is then stored in oak casks and left to mature, by law, for at least three years, but generally for five to eight years, in cool, dark, aromatic warehouses. It was these qualities that made Irish whiskey one of the favored drinks in both England and America at the beginning of the twentieth century.

But the heyday of Irish whiskey production would not last forever. From the days when John Jameson founded his distillery in Bow Street in 1780, through the period of political turmoil in Ireland (1916 to 1921) and Prohibition in America (1919 to 1933), the path did not always run smoothly. The distilling industry in Ireland withered for nearly four decades, until 1966, when the remaining whiskey distilleries joined forces to relaunch Irish whiskey in world markets. If the world was ever going to know the mellow warmth of Irish whiskey again, the Irish Distillers Group was determined to create that awareness.

For nearly two decades, Irish Distillers was alone in its efforts, producing well-known brands such as Jameson, John Power, Bushmills, and Paddy, as well as premium labels like Jameson 1780, Midleton Very Rare, and Bushmills 10-Year-Old Single Malt and Special Old Black Bush. Further expansion into the whiskey market arrived in 1987, when the Cooley Distillery of Dundalk, County Louth, came to an agreement with the owners of the old John Locke & Co. Distillery in Kilbeggan, County Westmeath. They refurbished and reopened the whiskey warehouse, installed a cooperage, and acquired the brand names of John Locke of Kilbeggan and Andrew A. Watt of Derry. In 1989, whiskey production resumed, and the first mature cask of Locke's Irish whiskey was tapped in July 1992. The following year, the Tyrconnell Single Malt Pure Pot Still brand was relaunched after an absence of fifty years, and Kilbeggan, a brand famous throughout Ireland in the nineteenth century, arrived in 1994.

The newest members of the Irish whiskey family are Knappogue Castle Single Malt, launched in 1997, and the Clontarf family of whiskeys, launched in 2005 by Castle Brands Inc., a New York importer. Knappogue Castle is bottled from casks of aged pot still whiskey that originated in the prestigious B. Daly Distillery in Tullamore, County Offaly. Clontarf, which is named after the famous Battle of Clontarf, where high king Brian Boru defeated the Viking army, consists of three premium whiskeys: Clontarf Irish, Clontarf Reserve, and Clontarf Single Malt.

Whichever brand you might choose for drinking, you can be assured of a clean, smooth, mellow, and smokeless taste. It's these same qualities that make Irish whiskey so appealing when used in cooking. The unique distillation recipe that produces the unmistakable, subtle taste of "Irish" is responsible for an unparalleled array of flavors in foods from traditional to contemporary. Simply put, a recipe built around a taste that took centuries to perfect is halfway there.

Previous spread, top: Lockes Distillery, Kilbeggan, County Westmeath
Previous spread, bottom: Pot still at Midleton Old Distillery, Midleton, County Cork

SMOKED SALMON and CRAB ROULADES with WALNUT VINAIGRETTE

I was first introduced to this smoked salmon roll-up, which makes an excellent starter or luncheon dish, at a small country house in Innishannon, County Cork. The original owners, Conal and Vera O'Sullivan, are no longer the proprietors, but their recipe remains one of my favorites. The earthy walnut vinaigrette nicely complements it.

SERVES 4 AS A STARTER

Walnut Vinaigrette	Roulades
3 tablespoons walnut oil	¾ cup mayonnaise
1 tablespoon canola oil	2 tablespoons Jameson Irish whiskey
1 tablespoon white wine vinegar	1 pound fresh crabmeat
Salt and freshly ground pepper	½ teaspoon fennel seeds
	8 thin slices smoked salmon (about 8 ounces), preferably Irish
	3 cups mixed salad greens
	1 avocado, peeled, pitted, and cut into 8 slices
	½ cup chopped walnuts
	Brown Soda Bread (page 81) for serving

To make the vinaigrette: Combine the oils, vinegar, and salt and pepper to taste in a sealable jar, cover, and shake until blended. Set aside.

To make the roulades: In a small bowl, whisk together the mayonnaise and whiskey. Stir in the crabmeat and fennel seeds. Spread the crabmeat mixture onto the slices of salmon, roll up into cylinder shapes, and refrigerate for 15 minutes.

To serve, divide the mixed greens among 4 salad plates. Place 2 roulades and 2 slices of avocado on each, and sprinkle with the walnuts. Drizzle the vinaigrette over the greens. Serve with Brown Soda Bread.

APPLE-WHISKEY PÂTÉ

The apple plays a prominent part in Irish legend and folklore, with its hues of green, gold, and russet inspiring tales and traditions that have been passed down for generations. Apples have always been a popular ingredient in Irish cookery, too, such as in this chicken liver pâté, where they are unexpected but surprisingly good. This recipe, which was once featured in a Dublin restaurant, blends apples and whiskey into the pâté to create an unusual flavor and texture.

SERVES 6 TO 8 AS A STARTER

¾ cup (1½ sticks) unsalted Kerrygold Irish butter

1 pound chicken livers, rinsed, dried, and coarsely chopped

¼ cup Irish whiskey

2 tablespoons minced onion

1 Granny Smith apple, peeled, cored, and chopped

2 tablespoons heavy (whipping) cream

1 teaspoon fresh lemon juice

Salt and freshly ground pepper

Fresh thyme sprigs for garnish

Buttered toast or crackers for serving

In a large skillet over medium heat, melt ¼ cup of the butter. Add the chicken livers and cook for 4 to 5 minutes, or until lightly browned. Add the whiskey, ignite, then allow the flame to burn out. Transfer the mixture to a food processor.

In the same skillet, melt ¼ cup more of the butter. Add the onion and apple and cook for 3 to 5 minutes, or until soft but not browned. Add the onion and apple mixture to the chicken livers and process for 20 to 30 seconds, or until smooth. Add the cream and process for 5 to 10 seconds, or until smooth. Let the mixture cool completely in the food processor.

Add the lemon juice, and salt and pepper to taste. Cut the remaining ¼ cup butter into small pieces and process, one piece at a time, until smooth. Press the mixture into a lightly oiled mold or small bowl, cover with plastic wrap, and refrigerate for several hours or overnight. At serving time, garnish with the thyme and serve with toast or crackers.

GAELIC STEAK

Many restaurants and pubs in Ireland serve steak with sautéed mushrooms and onions in whiskey sauce. At the Bridge House Hotel, in Tullamore, County Offaly, gaelic steak is their "house special." There it's made with Tullamore Dew whiskey, in honor of the distillery established in the town in 1829, but you can use your favorite brand with equally fine results. Serve it with Buttermilk-Chive Mashed Potatoes.

SERVES 4 AS A MAIN COURSE

2 tablespoons unsalted Kerrygold Irish butter

2 tablespoons extra-virgin olive oil

4 beef tenderloin steaks (filet mignon), 5 to 6 ounces each

1 clove garlic, minced

1 shallot, minced

4 ounces white mushrooms, chopped

1 teaspoon honey

½ teaspoon whole-grain mustard

2 tablespoons Irish whiskey

¾ cup homemade beef stock or canned low-sodium beef broth

¾ cup heavy (whipping) cream

Sea salt and freshly ground pepper

Fresh parsley sprigs for garnish

Buttermilk-Chive Mashed Potatoes (page 20) for serving

In a large skillet over medium heat, heat the butter and oil. Add the steaks and cook for 2 to 3 minutes on each side (for rare). Transfer the steaks to a warm plate and cover. Add the garlic, shallot, and mushrooms to the pan and cook for 2 to 3 minutes, or until soft but not browned. Stir in the honey and mustard and cook for 1 minute. Add the whiskey and stock or broth, and cook for 3 to 4 minutes, or until reduced by half. Whisk in the cream and cook for 2 to 3 minutes more, or until the sauce thickens. Season to taste with salt and pepper.

To serve, place each steak on a serving plate and spoon some of the sauce over the top. Garnish with the parsley and serve with the potatoes.

BUSHMILLS DUCK au POIVRE

Paul Rankin, who grew up in Ballywalter, County Down, is one of Northern Ireland's most well-known chefs. Together with his wife, Jeanne, they operate Cayenne, a fashionable Belfast restaurant in Shaftesbury Square; Café Paul Rankin, with numerous locations throughout Northern Ireland; and Rain City, a casual bistro situated in the Queen's University quarter of Belfast. In 2004, he teamed up with another Northern Ireland native, Bushmills Irish whiskey, becoming its official international ambassador to promote the brand for drinking and cooking. This peppered duck with whiskey sauce is one of several recipes he created to showcase the brand. Serve the duck with Potato, Parsnip, and Apple Purée with Parsnip Crisps.

SERVES 4 AS A MAIN COURSE

---

4 duck breasts, 6 to 7 ounces each, skin removed

2 tablespoons freshly ground pepper

Sea salt

1 tablespoon canola oil

1 tablespoon unsalted Kerrygold Irish butter

1 tablespoon sherry vinegar

1 tablespoon minced shallot

¼ cup homemade beef stock or canned low-sodium beef broth

¼ cup Bushmills Irish whiskey

¾ cup heavy (whipping) cream

Potato, Parsnip, and Apple Purée with Parsnip Crisps (page 22) for serving

---

Rub both sides of the duck breasts with the pepper, pressing it into the flesh with your fingers. Season with salt.

In a large skillet over medium-high heat, heat the oil and butter. Add the duck and cook for 3 minutes on each side (for medium rare; 6 minutes per side for well done). Remove the duck from the pan and keep warm. Add the vinegar and shallot, and, with a wooden spoon, scrape up the browned bits from the bottom of the pan. Stir in the stock or broth, whiskey, and cream, reduce the heat to low, and simmer for 5 to 7 minutes, or until the sauce thickens.

To serve, slice each duck breast and arrange on a warmed serving plate. Surround with the sauce and serve with the purée. Sprinkle the parsnip crisps on top.

BUTTERMILK-CHIVE MASHED POTATOES

SERVES 4 TO 6 AS A SIDE DISH

3 pounds baking potatoes, peeled and cut into 1-inch pieces

½ cup (1 stick) unsalted Kerrygold Irish butter, cut into pieces

1 cup buttermilk

¼ cup half-and-half

½ teaspoon dried thyme

3 tablespoons minced fresh chives

Salt and freshly ground pepper

Cook the potatoes in a large pot of boiling salted water for 15 to 18 minutes, or until tender. Drain, then return them to the pot to dry out a little. Mash over low heat until almost smooth. Stir in the butter, buttermilk, half-and-half, thyme, and chives. Season to taste with salt and pepper.

CARROT and TURNIP PURÉE

SERVES 4 TO 6 AS A SIDE DISH

2 pounds carrots, peeled and cut into pieces

2 pounds turnips, peeled and cut into pieces

½ cup sour cream

¼ teaspoon ground ginger

4 tablespoons unsalted Kerrygold Irish butter, at room temperature

Salt and freshly ground pepper

Minced fresh chives for garnish

Cook the carrots and turnips in salted boiling water for 30 to 40 minutes, or until tender. Drain and mash. Transfer to a food processor. Add the sour cream, ginger, and butter and process for 15 to 20 seconds, or until smooth. Season to taste with salt and pepper and sprinkle with the chives.

CRUSHED POTATOES

SERVES **6 TO 8** AS A SIDE DISH

2 pounds small potatoes (fingerlings, Yukon Gold, or Red Bliss), unpeeled

2 tablespoons unsalted Kerrygold Irish butter, cut into pieces

2 tablespoons extra-virgin olive oil

3 tablespoons crumbled blue cheese or 1 table-spoon whole-grain mustard (optional)

Sea salt and freshly ground pepper

Cook the potatoes in a large pot of boiling salted water for about 30 minutes, or until tender, and drain. Return them to the same pot to dry out a little. With a wooden spoon, roughly crush the potatoes. Stir in the butter, oil, and cheese or mustard, if using. Season to taste with salt and pepper.

BOILED NEW POTATOES

SERVES **6 TO 8** AS A SIDE DISH

3 pounds small white unpeeled potatoes

2 tablespoons unsalted Kerrygold Irish butter

½ cup minced fresh flat-leaf parsley

Salt and freshly ground pepper

Cook the potatoes in salted boiling water for 12 to 15 minutes, or until tender. Drain and return to the pan to dry out a little. Top with the butter, parsley, and salt and pepper to taste. Serve hot.

POTATO, PARSNIP, and APPLE PURÉE with PARSNIP CRISPS

SERVES 6 TO 8 AS A SIDE DISH

2 pounds parsnips (reserve 1 parsnip for Parsnip Crisps), peeled and cut into 1-inch pieces	½ cup water
2 tablespoons canola oil	1½ pounds Granny Smith apples, peeled, cored, and sliced
Salt and freshly ground pepper	2 cups milk
2 pounds baking potatoes, peeled and cut into 1-inch pieces	1 cup (2 sticks) plus 2 tablespoons unsalted Kerrygold Irish butter, cut into pieces

To make the Parsnip Crisps: Using a vegetable peeler, peel 1 large parsnip, then continue cutting it into long, thin strips. Spread the strips out on a paper towel to dry slightly. In a large skillet over medium heat, heat 2 tablespoons canola oil. Fry the strips in batches for 2 to 3 minutes, or until they twist up and are crisp. With a slotted spoon, transfer to paper towels to drain. Sprinkle with salt and pepper.

Cook the parsnips and potatoes in a large saucepan of salted boiling water for 20 to 25 minutes, or until tender. Drain and mash. Return to the saucepan. Meanwhile, in a medium saucepan, bring the water to a simmer over low heat. Add the apples, cover, and cook for 20 to 25 minutes, or until soft. Drain and mash.

Combine the mashed apples with the mashed potatoes and parsnips in a pot. In a medium saucepan, bring the milk to a boil over medium heat. Add the milk and butter to the vegetable mixture and, using a handheld electric mixer or immersion blender, blend until smooth. Stir over medium heat until heated through. Season to taste with salt and pepper and sprinkle with the Parsnip Crisps.

HONEY-GLAZED BACON
with APPLE-WHISKEY SAUCE

The distinctive flavor of Irish whiskey in sauces, for basting, and for marinating combines beautifully with a variety of meats, such as this loin of bacon, which is boiled first, then baked with honey and mustard and served with an apple cream sauce. It's a great party dish because it can be prepared ahead of time and served cold with the warm sauce. Serve with Buttermilk-Chive Mashed Potatoes.

SERVES 4 TO 6 AS A MAIN COURSE

Honey-Glazed Bacon

1 loin of bacon, 3 to 4 pounds
(see Resources, page 151)

2 stalks celery, chopped

1 carrot, chopped

1 or 2 bay leaves

1 teaspoon black peppercorns

1 tablespoon whole-grain mustard

1 tablespoon honey

Apple-Whiskey Sauce

1 tablespoon unsalted Kerrygold Irish butter

3 Granny Smith apples, peeled, cored, and sliced

¼ cup reserved cooking liquid

2 tablespoons Irish whiskey

3 tablespoons heavy (whipping) cream

1 tablespoon minced fresh tarragon

Salt and freshly ground pepper

Buttermilk-Chive Mashed Potatoes
(page 20) for serving

In a large pot of cold water, bring the bacon, celery, carrot, bay leaves, and peppercorns to a boil. Reduce the heat to low, cover, and simmer, skimming the water occasionally to remove any foam that rises, for 60 to 75 minutes, or until the meat is fork-tender (approximately 30 minutes per pound).

Preheat the oven to 400°F. Transfer the bacon to a roasting pan, straining and reserving the liquid. Remove the rind and score the fat. In a small bowl, whisk together the mustard and honey. Spread it over the bacon. Add ⅔ cup of the cooking liquid to the roasting pan and bake, basting occasionally, for 20 minutes. Add more liquid to the pan if necessary during cooking. Transfer to a serving plate.

To make the sauce: In a small saucepan over medium heat, melt the butter. Add the apple slices and cook for 5 minutes, or until golden. Add ¼ cup of the cooking liquid, the whiskey, and cream, and boil for 3 to 5 minutes, stirring continuously, or until the sauce begins to thicken. Add the tarragon, and season to taste with salt and pepper. To serve, slice the meat and serve with the sauce and potatoes.

CHICKEN CASHEL BLUE

Cashel Blue cheese, Ireland's first farmhouse blue, is a mild cheese with a distinctive flavor and a creamy texture. It's one of the country's best-known farmhouse cheeses, and it consistently appears in recipes in fine hotels and restaurants and on cheeseboards. Jane and Louis Grubb make this cheese in Fethard, County Tipperary, near the famous Rock of Cashel. In this recipe, which originated at a local restaurant, the cheese is used to stuff chicken breasts, which are finished with a whiskey and mushroom sauce. Serve with Carrot and Turnip Purée.

SERVES 4 AS A MAIN COURSE

---

4 boneless chicken breast halves,
4 to 5 ounces each

4 ounces Cashel Blue cheese

½ cup all-purpose flour

1 large egg beaten with 1 tablespoon milk

½ cup fresh white bread crumbs (see Note)

2 tablespoons canola oil

2 tablespoons extra-virgin olive oil

3 tablespoons minced shallot

6 ounces white mushrooms, chopped

2 tablespoons Irish whiskey

¼ cup half-and-half

Salt and freshly ground pepper

Fresh watercress for garnish

Carrot and Turnip Purée
(page 20) for serving

Preheat the oven to 350°F. Make a horizontal incision in each chicken breast to form a pocket. Cut the cheese into 4 pieces, and roll each piece into a cylinder shape. Stuff one into each chicken breast pocket.

Put the flour in one shallow dish, the egg wash in another, and the bread crumbs in a third. Lightly dredge each piece of chicken in the flour, dip in the egg wash, and then cover with bread crumbs. Refrigerate for 15 minutes.

In a large skillet over medium heat, heat the canola oil. Cook the chicken for 3 to 5 minutes on each side, or until lightly browned. Transfer to a casserole dish and bake for 10 to 15 minutes while preparing the sauce.

In another skillet over medium heat, heat the olive oil. Add the shallot and mushrooms and cook for 3 to 5 minutes, or until soft but not browned. Add the whiskey and cook for 2 to 3 minutes, or until slightly reduced. Stir in the half-and-half, season to taste with salt and pepper, and cook for 2 to 3 minutes longer, or until smooth.

To serve, place a chicken breast in the center of each of 4 plates and spoon the sauce over the top. Garnish with the watercress and serve with the purée.

Note: To make fresh bread crumbs, cut 5 to 6 slices of a stale baguette or rustic bread into ½-inch cubes. Put in a blender or a food processor. Process for 15 to 20 seconds, or until the mixture is ground into fine crumbs.

Irish Whiskey History

Historians claim that Irish whiskey was the elixir that cured the sick in the Dark Ages and gave strength to soldiers in the Middle Ages. Artists and writers have called it the nectar that loosens the creativity of playwrights, the voices of singers, and the fingers of musicians. When James Joyce heard "the light music of whiskey falling into a glass," he called it a "most agreeable interlude." Even Russian czar Peter the Great developed a fondness for Irish whiskey and declared, "Of all wines, the Irish spirit is the best."

Irish whiskey distilling today takes place in several locations around Ireland, producing some of the world's most famous brands of blended and single malt whiskeys. (Single malt whiskeys are those that are made only from malted barley from a single distillery.) In addition to Jameson, which dominates the industry, Bushmills produces three single malts—Bushmills 10-Year-Old, Bushmills 12-Year-Old Reserve, and Bushmills 16-Year-Old Three-Wood—along with some whiskeys that are blended with Irish grain whiskey—Bushmills Original, Black Bush, and Bushmills 1608. Other well-known whiskeys (some of which are available only in Ireland) are Tullamore Dew, Paddy, John Power, Redbreast, and Midleton Very Rare; Locke's, Tyrconnell Single Malt, Kilbeggan, and Connemara Peated Single Malt, from Cooleys Distillery, in Dundalk, County Louth; Knappogue Castle Single Malt and a new Clontarf range of three premium whiskeys, both from Castle Brands.

In Ireland, there are five whiskey museum/visitor centers that provide tours and tastings: the Old Jameson Distillery, Bow Street, Dublin; the Jameson Heritage Center, Midleton, County Cork; the Old Bushmills Distillery, Bushmills, County Antrim; Tullamore Dew Heritage Center, Tullamore, County Offaly; and Locke's Distillery Museum, Kilbeggan, County Westmeath. (See Resources, page 151.)

CHOPS in LOCKE'S

Clever cooks often marinate meat in an alcohol-based product to tenderize it and add flavor. Lamb chops are perfect for this technique, especially less expensive chops like shoulder (round bone or blade), which are also perfect for outdoor grilling. This marinade uses Locke's Irish whiskey and plenty of thyme, "that chief of seasoners," according to James Joyce, who likened history to an Irish stew, influenced by thyme! Marinate the chops for at least 12 hours before you plan to grill them. Serve with Crushed Potatoes and a mixed green salad.

SERVES 6 AS A MAIN COURSE

½ cup Locke's Irish whiskey

¾ cup olive oil

1 clove garlic, minced

1 small onion, chopped

2 sprigs fresh thyme

1 sprig fresh rosemary

¼ teaspoon cayenne pepper

Salt and freshly ground pepper

One ½-inch piece fresh ginger, peeled and grated

6 lamb cutlets, chops, or steaks, 4 to 6 ounces each

Crushed Potatoes (page 21) for serving

Combine the whiskey, oil, garlic, onion, thyme, rosemary, cayenne, salt and pepper to taste, and ginger in a sealable jar and shake to blend. Place the lamb in a shallow dish and pour the marinade over it. Cover and refrigerate for at least 12 hours.

Prepare a medium-hot fire in a charcoal grill, preheat a gas grill to medium-high, or preheat the broiler. Remove the lamb from the marinade. Grill, or broil 4 inches from the heat source, for 5 minutes on each side (for rare). Brush once with the marinade after turning. Serve immediately with the potatoes and a green salad.

LAMB FOLLÁIN

Folláin Irish whiskey marmalade is made from the finest natural ingredients—Seville and sweet oranges, lemons, and sugar—and fortified with Jameson Irish whiskey. Delicious on toast, biscuits, and scones, it's also wonderful in combination with other ingredients in marinades and sauces, and as a coating for leg of lamb. Folláin (from the Irish word meaning "wholesomeness") preserves, marmalades, jams, and chutneys are made by Peadar and Maureen Ó Lionáid in Ballyvourney, in the Gaeltacht (Irish-speaking area) of County Cork. Their products contain no artificial preservatives or colorings. Serve this roast lamb with Rutabaga Purée or Turnip Gratin.

SERVES 6 TO 8 AS A MAIN COURSE

---

3 tablespoons Folláin orange whiskey marmalade or similar orange whiskey marmalade

2 tablespoons Irish whiskey

2 tablespoons grated orange zest

2 tablespoons minced garlic

3 tablespoons olive oil

½ cup orange juice

3 tablespoons minced fresh chives

Salt and freshly ground pepper

1 leg of lamb, 5 to 7 pounds

Rutabaga Purée (page 113) or Turnip Gratin (page 108) for serving

---

In a small saucepan over medium heat, combine the marmalade, whiskey, orange zest, garlic, oil, orange juice, chives, and salt and pepper to taste. Cook for 5 to 8 minutes, or until the marmalade melts and the sauce is smooth.

Place the lamb in a shallow dish and pour the marinade over it, reserving ¼ cup for basting. Turn to coat, cover, and refrigerate for at least 12 hours, or up to 24 hours. Turn the lamb 2 to 3 times during marinating to coat it evenly. Remove the lamb from the refrigerator and let it sit at room temperature for 1 hour.

Preheat the oven to 325°F. Remove the lamb from the marinade and pat it dry. Place it in a roasting pan and cook, basting 2 or 3 times with the reserved marinade, for 2½ to 3 hours, or until a thermometer inserted into the thickest part of the lamb registers 170°F (medium rare), 175°F (medium), or 180°F (well done). Transfer the lamb to a serving platter and let it rest for 15 minutes before carving.

In a large bowl, beat the butter and granulated sugar with an electric mixer for 4 to 5 minutes, or until light and fluffy. Add the egg and beat until smooth. Fold in the flour mixture alternately with the reserved liquid. Stir in the raisins, walnuts, and whiskey.

Pour into the prepared pans. Bake for 30 to 35 minutes, or until a skewer inserted in the center comes out clean. Remove from the oven and let cool in the pans for 15 minutes. Invert the pans onto a wire rack, remove the wax paper, then set the cakes upright. Let cool completely.

To make the icing: In a large bowl, beat the butter and confectioners' sugar with an electric mixer for 2 to 3 minutes, or until smooth. Add the egg and whiskey and beat until smooth. With a spatula, spread a third of the icing onto the top of one of the layers. Place the second layer on top, and spread the top and sides with the remaining icing. Garnish with walnut halves, if desired. Let the icing set for 15 to 20 minutes before cutting the cake into slices.

Irish Coffee

In 1943, chef-barman Joe Sheridan decided that a blend of cream, hot coffee, and Irish whiskey would make a perfect welcoming drink for cold and weary passengers arriving at the town of Foynes, in County Limerick, from the United States on the "flying boats," the first transatlantic passenger planes. He wanted the drink to be warm and welcoming, Irish in character, and sophisticated enough to appeal to international travelers. After many experiments over a number of years, including the addition of sugar, Sheridan finally came up with the recipe for what would become the quintessential Irish drink. When Shannon International Airport opened in 1947, Irish coffee became its official beverage.

In the early 1950s, *San Francisco Chronicle* journalist Stan Delaplane enjoyed an Irish coffee at Shannon and introduced it to America at his favorite watering hole, the Buena Vista Café near Fisherman's Wharf. Irish coffee soon became the favorite drink of San Francisco. Since its introduction in 1952, more than 15 million have been served at that popular café alone, and millions more elsewhere.

Joe Sheridan's original recipe, which is still used at the Buena Vista, is as follows: Heat a stemmed, heatproof goblet by running it under very hot water. Pour in 1 jigger of Irish whiskey. Add 3 cubes of sugar and fill the goblet with strong black coffee to within 1 inch of the brim. Stir to dissolve the sugar. Top off with lightly whipped cream. Do not stir after adding the cream, as the true flavor is obtained by drinking the hot mixture through the cream. *Sláinte!*

HOT IRISHMAN MERINGUES

Hot Irishman is a blend of single malt Irish whiskey, Irish brown sugar, and Colombian coffee. To make a perfect Irish coffee, you just need to add boiling water and lightly whipped cream. The drink was conceived by husband-and-wife team Bernard and Rosemary Walsh, who blend and bottle their product in Ireland, allowing it to mature over time to marry the flavors. It's a convenient way to make Irish coffee for drinking or for use in recipes calling for it, such as these meringues, which are filled with whipped cream. You can add some fresh berries, if you wish.

SERVES 8 (EACH MERINGUE SERVES 4)

Meringues	Filling
2 large egg whites	1¼ cups heavy (whipping) cream
¾ cup plus 2 tablespoons confectioners' sugar	2 tablespoons Hot Irishman
2 teaspoons Hot Irishman (see Resources, page 151)	
	Sliced strawberries for garnish (optional)

To make the meringues: Preheat the oven to 250°F. Line a baking sheet with parchment or wax paper. For uniform meringues, draw two 7-inch circles onto the paper. Set aside.

In the large bowl of a stand mixer fitted with a whisk, combine the egg whites and ¾ cup of the confectioners' sugar. Beat for 10 to 12 minutes, or until firm, dry peaks form. In a separate bowl, whisk the Hot Irishman with the remaining 2 tablespoons sugar and gently fold into the egg whites. With a palette knife, spread the meringue onto the circles. Depress the center of each with a spoon to create a hollow. Bake for 1½ to 2 hours, or until the meringues are dry and crisp. Turn off the oven and let them cool completely. When cooled, slide a spatula or knife between them and the paper to separate them. (Meringues can be stored in an airtight container for up to 1 week.)

To make the filling: In a large bowl, whip the cream until stiff peaks form. Whisk in the Hot Irishman. Spoon the whipped cream into the center of each meringue and, if you desire, top with a few strawberry slices.

BUSHMILLS MARMALADE PUDDINGS

The whiskeys produced at the Old Bushmills Distillery are counted among the finest in the world. At the Bushmills Inn, a lovely hotel that was once a stagecoach stop, the chef serves old-fashioned marmalade puddings as a tribute to the nearby distillery. If you want a stronger whiskey flavor, use Irish whiskey marmalade, such as Folláin brand, which is made in Ballyvourney, County Cork.

SERVES 6

13 tablespoons thick-cut orange marmalade

1½ cups (3 sticks) unsalted Kerrygold Irish butter, at room temperature

1½ cups superfine sugar

6 large eggs, beaten

Grated zest of 2 oranges

3 cups self-rising flour

1½ teaspoons ground allspice

Crème Anglaise (page 42) for serving

Orange segments for garnish

Mint sprigs for garnish

Preheat the oven to 325°F. Generously grease six 8-ounce ramekins. Put 2 tablespoons of marmalade in the bottom of each.

In a large bowl, beat the butter and sugar with an electric mixer until light and fluffy. Add the eggs, orange zest, and the remaining 1 tablespoon marmalade. Gradually beat in the flour and allspice. Spoon into the prepared ramekins. Put the ramekins in a large baking pan and add enough hot water to the pan to come halfway up the sides of the dishes. Cover the pan with wax paper, then with aluminum foil, and prick the foil in 6 to 8 places. Bake for 25 to 30 minutes, or until the puddings are set and lightly browned. Remove from the oven.

To serve, divide the crème anglaise among 6 serving plates. Run a knife around the edge of each ramekin and invert the puddings onto the plates. Garnish each with orange segments and a sprig of mint.

MOCHA SOUFFLÉS
with CHOCOLATE WHISKEY SAUCE

A light, perfectly risen soufflé is always an impressive dessert, and when it assumes the flavor of Irish coffee, it's irresistible. With two forks, pull open the tops of the soufflés and spoon the creamy whiskey sauce into the center of each one.

SERVES 6

Soufflés	Chocolate Whiskey Sauce
2 tablespoons ground hazelnuts or almonds	²/₃ cup heavy (whipping) cream
5 ounces semisweet chocolate, broken into pieces	4 ounces semisweet chocolate, broken into pieces
¼ cup freshly brewed coffee	2 tablespoons Irish whiskey
2 teaspoons all-purpose flour	
¼ cup sugar	Vanilla ice cream for serving
4 large eggs, separated	

To make the soufflés: Preheat the oven to 375°F. Butter six 8-ounce ramekins and dust with the ground nuts, shaking out the excess.

In a large microwave-safe bowl, combine the chocolate and coffee. Microwave on medium (50 percent) for 2 to 2½ minutes, or until melted. Alternately, melt the chocolate over a pan of simmering water, then add the coffee. Stir the flour, 2 tablespoons of the sugar, and the egg yolks into the chocolate mixture.

In a large bowl, beat the egg whites with an electric mixer until soft peaks form. Sprinkle in the remaining 2 tablespoons sugar and beat until stiff peaks form. Fold one quarter of the egg whites into the chocolate mixture to lighten it, then gently fold in the remaining egg whites. Spoon into the prepared ramekins, and bake for 15 to 20 minutes, or until the tops are risen and firm. Remove from the oven and let cool on a wire rack for 5 minutes.

To make the sauce: In a small saucepan over medium-low heat, heat the cream. Remove from the heat, stir in the chocolate, and whisk until smooth. Whisk in the whiskey.

To serve, split open the top of each soufflé with forks, spoon in some sauce, and top with a scoop of ice cream.

JAMESON CHOCOLATE-WALNUT-CARAMEL TART

In the two hundred years since it was first produced, Jameson has become the world's leading Irish whiskey. As one of the fastest-growing international spirits, Irish whiskey is also making its mark on Irish cookery, especially in desserts, where its distinctive taste complements a wide range of flavors. The combination of whiskey and chocolate is especially delicious, and when nuts and caramel are added, as in this tart, the results are superb.

SERVES 8

Crust

1¼ cups all-purpose flour

1 teaspoon granulated sugar

¼ teaspoon salt

4 tablespoons cold unsalted Kerrygold Irish butter, cut into small pieces

4 tablespoons cold vegetable shortening, cut into small pieces

3 to 4 tablespoons ice water

Caramel Sauce

4 tablespoons unsalted Kerrygold Irish butter

½ cup granulated sugar

¼ cup heavy (whipping) cream

Filling

1 cup chopped walnuts

½ cup coarsely chopped bittersweet (not unsweetened) or semisweet chocolate

¾ cup light corn syrup

½ cup packed light brown sugar

½ cup packed dark brown sugar

4 tablespoons unsalted Kerrygold Irish butter, cut into pieces

3 large eggs

3 tablespoons Jameson Irish whiskey

1 teaspoon vanilla extract

¼ teaspoon salt

Confectioners' sugar for dusting

To make the crust: Combine the flour, granulated sugar, and salt in a food processor fitted with a metal blade. Add the butter and shortening and pulse 8 to 12 times, or until the mixture resembles coarse crumbs. Add 2 tablespoons of the water and process for 15 to 20 seconds, or until the dough comes together. Add the remaining water if necessary, and pulse again. Dust a work surface with flour. Turn out the dough, form it into a ball, then wrap it in plastic wrap and refrigerate for 1 hour. Remove the dough from the refrigerator 10 minutes before rolling.

Butter a 10-inch tart pan with a removable bottom. Dust a work surface with flour. Roll out the dough to a circle 12 inches in diameter. Transfer to the prepared pan, fold in the excess dough, and press with your fingers to form thick sides. Freeze for 30 minutes, or until firm.

Preheat the oven to 375°F. Prick the bottom and sides of the crust with a fork. Line the crust with aluminum foil, fill with pie weights or dry beans, and bake for 20 minutes. Remove the weights and foil and bake for 12 to 15 minutes more, or until the crust is browned all over. Remove from the oven and let cool on a wire rack. Maintain the oven temperature.

To make the caramel sauce: In a saucepan over medium heat, combine the butter and granulated sugar. Cook, stirring constantly, for 3 to 5 minutes, or until the mixture thickens. Continue cooking until the mixture turns golden brown. Remove from the heat and stir in the cream. Pour the caramel mixture into the tart crust, spread it evenly over the bottom, and freeze for 15 minutes, or until set.

To make the filling: Sprinkle half of the walnuts and all of the chocolate pieces over the caramel. In a large bowl, beat the corn syrup, brown sugars, butter, eggs, whiskey, vanilla, and salt with an electric mixer until smooth. Pour over the chocolate and walnuts. Sprinkle the remaining half of the walnuts over the top. Bake the tart for about 50 minutes, or until the filling is nearly set in the center. Remove from the oven and let cool on a wire rack for 10 minutes. Release the side of the pan. Dust with confectioners' sugar, slice the tart, and serve it warm.

OATMEAL-WHISKEY CRÈMES BRÛLÉES with STRAWBERRY-RHUBARB COMPOTE

Many Irish chefs are invited each year to cook in James Beard's kitchen at the Greenwich Village townhouse where his culinary foundation is now located. A few years ago, Patrick McLarnon, currently executive chef at Francesca's, at the Brooks Hotel, in Dublin, served this traditional crème brûlée for dessert. He gave it a distinctive Irish touch by adding toasted steel-cut oats and Irish whiskey. The compote is a tribute to spring, but you can vary the fruit to suit what's in season.

SERVES 6

Crèmes Brûlées	Strawberry-Rhubarb Compote
2 tablespoons McCann's steel-cut Irish oats (see Resources, page 151)	1¼ cups water
2 tablespoons Irish whiskey	1½ cups sugar
5 large egg yolks	1 pound rhubarb, cut into 1-inch pieces
½ cup plus 1 tablespoon sugar	2 cups hulled, sliced strawberries
2 cups heavy (whipping) cream	

To make the crèmes brûlées: Preheat the oven to 375°F. Butter six 6-ounce ramekins.

Place the oats in a shallow baking dish and toast in the oven for about 10 minutes, or until browned. Remove from the oven and pour the whiskey over the oats; it will evaporate from the heat of the pan. Reduce the heat to 325°F.

In a small bowl, whisk the egg yolks and ½ cup of the sugar together. Stir in the cream and toasted oats. Spoon into the prepared ramekins. Set the ramekins in a large baking pan and add enough hot water to come halfway up the sides of the dishes. Bake for 45 to 50 minutes, or until the custard is set. Remove from the oven and let cool in the pan for 15 minutes. Remove the ramekins from the pan, cover with plastic wrap, and refrigerate until serving time.

To make the compote: In a small saucepan over medium heat, bring the water and sugar to a boil. Cook for 2 to 3 minutes, or until slightly syrupy. Reduce the heat to low, add the rhubarb and strawberries, and simmer for 10 minutes, or until the fruit is tender. Remove from the heat and let cool completely. Cover and refrigerate.

To serve: Preheat the broiler. Sprinkle each custard with some of the remaining 1 tablespoon sugar. Place under the broiler 4 inches from the heat for 1 to 2 minutes, or use a kitchen blowtorch and move the flame constantly over the surface until the sugar melts, bubbles, and lightly browns. Serve with the compote alongside.

Fitzpatricks Pub and Restaurant, Rockmarshall, County Louth

POITÍN ICE CREAM

SERVES 4 TO 6

1½ cups heavy (whipping) cream	1 tablespoon poitín (see facing page)
1 teaspoon ground cinnamon	⅓ cup confectioners' sugar, sifted
2 cups Crème Anglaise (see Note)	

In a medium saucepan over medium heat, combine the cream and cinnamon. Bring nearly to a boil, then remove from the heat and let cool for 30 minutes.

In a large bowl, combine the crème anglaise and poitín. Whisk in the confectioners' sugar. Whisk the cream mixture into the custard mixture and let it cool for 1 hour. Refrigerate for 2 hours.

Process in a 1-quart ice cream maker according to the manufacturer's directions. Transfer to a plastic container and freeze until firm.

Note: The recipe for Crème Anglaise (below) contains whiskey. For this recipe, omit it, or make Crème Anglaise using custard powder such as Bird's (see Resources, page 151).

CRÈME ANGLAISE

MAKES 2 CUPS

1 cup heavy (whipping) cream	½ cup superfine sugar
1 cup whole milk	3 tablespoons Irish whiskey
5 large egg yolks	1 teaspoon vanilla extract

In a heavy saucepan, combine the cream and milk over medium heat and bring to a simmer. In a medium bowl, whisk the egg yolks and sugar together. Gradually whisk the hot milk into the egg yolks. Return the egg yolk mixture to the pan and whisk constantly over medium heat for 6 to 8 minutes, or until the custard thickens enough to coat the back of a spoon. Transfer to a bowl and whisk in the whiskey and vanilla. Place a piece of plastic wrap over the top to prevent a skin from forming, and let cool. Refrigerate until serving time.

Poitín

The clear liquid known as poitín (pronounced "potcheen") is a drink of many names. Some have called it "the Connemara Doctor," "Irish Moonshine," and even "Mountain Dew." The name is actually derived from the Irish word meaning "little pot," and is so called because it was distilled in pot stills in remote mountain areas of the country. Poitín is frequently a water-clear distillation of barley, sugar, yeast, and pure mountain water. As in the production of whiskey, barley is steeped in water until it sprouts, and then it is dried. Later, it is boiled and distilled through what's known as a "worm," a large, spiraling coil. Traditionally, the manufacture of the fiery brew took place up in the hills close to the source of Ireland's crystal clear streams.

Poitín's medicinal moniker ("the Connemara Doctor") comes from the fact that it was frequently used as a cure for all sorts of ills. Greyhounds reportedly ran faster when poitín was rubbed onto their limbs, and horses apparently jumped higher hurdles when administered likewise. Some even claim that a fighting cock won the All-Ireland Championship along the Cavan border in 1947 because his blood was fired with poitín! Poitín is also administered orally, the preference for most human consumption!

Since the beginning of time, the Irish have been dedicated distillers. The introduction of an excise duty in 1661 led the authorities to seek ways of simplifying tax collection. Regulation was designed to encourage the use of large commercial stills. These were operated by companies that formed the basis of the Irish whiskey industry today. No amount of regulation, however, could persuade the Irish to give up the virtues of the small pot, and while it has been illegal since 1661, the craft of small pot distilling still goes on in remote areas of Ireland.

Bunratty Potcheen has all the taste characteristics of authentic poitín and is produced by a unique process at Bunratty Winery in County Clare. In 1989, the company was granted a license from the Irish government to produce it for export only, and in 1997, it was legalized for sale in the Irish domestic market. The product of the small pot is now legally available for all to enjoy.

Knockeen Hills Irish Poteen, grain-based and triple-distilled in County Waterford, is another poitín to look for. Like other fine Irish spirits, it's equally exciting in cooking and can be used in most recipes calling for Irish whiskey.

BROWN BREAD APPLE COBBLER

Oatmeal-topped cobblers and crisps are real crowd-pleasers, and they're easy on the cook, too, because they can be made in advance and reheated at serving time. This cobbler substitutes brown soda bread crumbs for the usual oatmeal, and offers two snappy toppings: a whiskey-flavored crème anglaise and a poitín-spiked cinnamon ice cream that is similar to a commercially made one that uses Knockeen Hills Irish Poteen (see page 43). Start to prepare the cobbler about an hour ahead to allow enough time to plump up the raisins.

SERVES 6 TO 8

⅓ cup water	2 cups Brown Soda Bread crumbs (see page 81)
5 tablespoons Irish whiskey	6 tablespoons unsalted Kerrygold Irish butter, melted
⅓ cup golden raisins	
1 teaspoon vanilla extract	½ cup packed light brown sugar
4 large Granny Smith apples, peeled, cored, and cut into ½-inch pieces	½ teaspoon ground cinnamon
	Crème Anglaise (page 42) or Poitín Ice Cream (page 42) for serving
⅓ cup granulated sugar	

In a small saucepan over medium heat, bring the water and whiskey to a boil. Stir in the raisins and vanilla. Remove from the heat, cover, and let stand for 1 hour, or until the raisins have absorbed most of the liquid.

Preheat the oven to 375°F. Butter an 8- or 9-inch square glass baking dish.

In a large bowl, toss the apples with the granulated sugar. Stir in the raisins and cooking liquid.

In a medium bowl, combine the bread crumbs, butter, brown sugar, and cinnamon. Transfer half the apple mixture to the prepared dish. Top with half the bread crumb mixture. Repeat the layers with the remaining apples and bread crumbs. Bake for 50 to 55 minutes, or until the apples are tender, the filling is bubbling, and the topping is browned and crisp. Remove from the oven and cool on a wire rack for about 10 minutes. Serve topped with the crème anglaise or poitín ice cream.

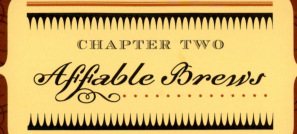

CHAPTER TWO

Affable Brews

The art of brewing may have been born as long ago as six thousand years. Hieroglyphics have been found that seem to symbolize brewing, and some evidence of beer has been recorded in all languages. Next to water and wine, beer is possibly the universal drink of mankind. Ancient humans discovered that by harvesting the fruits of the earth—wild-growing, sugar-containing raw materials such as grapes, fruits, berries, and honey—adding water, and leaving the mixture exposed to the warmth of airborne natural yeasts, they could produce a stimulating beverage. In those areas where starchy grasses like wheat, barley, and rye grew, the beverage came to be known as *bouzah*, after the old city of Bousiris, in the Nile Delta.

The technique of brewing eventually spread across Europe to the green and fertile land of Ireland, where Neolithic inhabitants began to sow the seeds of an Irish brewing tradition by planting wheat and barley. From the fifth century, when Saint Patrick reportedly traveled around Ireland with his own brewer, a priest called Mescan, to the great Saint Brigid, who did the brewing for all the churches in the Kildare area, brewing grew as an important art in medieval Ireland.

In late 1759, Kildare-born Arthur Guinness decided to "try his luck in Dublin," where he took out a nine-thousand-year lease on a small, unused, ill-equipped brewery at St. James's Gate, hoping to make it prosper. After first brewing ale, Guinness found that he would have to compete with a new drink popular with the porters at Covent Garden and Billingsgate, which was being exported to Dublin by London brewers. Tackling the English brewers at their own game, Guinness tried his hand at the new "porter" and established a tradition that is, perhaps, unsurpassed in brewing history.

The characteristic dark color of porter, which is made with a top-fermenting yeast, is the result of using roasted barley in addition to hops and water. Determined to brew a better porter than his competitors, in 1822 Guinness laid down exact regulations for the brewing of "Extra Superior Porter." The word "stout," meaning "hearty" and "robust," was added in the early 1920s as an adjective describing porter, but the word evolved into a name in its own right. Today the world is blessed with several Irish stouts in addition to the original Guinness.

Murphy's Irish stout, brewed at Lady's Well Brewery in Cork City, is the result of the energy and enterprise of the four Murphy brothers, James, William, Jerome, and Francis, who founded the family business in 1856. In the nineteenth century, Cork City was considered to be an excellent location for a brewery, since it was close to the finest malting barley from the country's limestone soils and pure Cork water. This combination continues to be responsible for the creamy, mellow flavor of Murphy's Irish stout. The brewery is now owned by Heineken Ireland.

Beamish & Crawford was founded by two Cork merchants in 1792 to compete with the increasing importation of London porters. Like other brewers who began with ale, William Beamish and William Crawford started brewing porter at Cramer's Lane in Cork, site of part of the present brewery, and have continued that tradition for two centuries.

John Smithwick founded his brewery in 1710 at St. Francis Abbey, in the medieval city of Kilkenny. He was one of the first to brew ale, a drink made with top-fermenting yeast. Ample supplies of soft water from the nearby Nore and Breagagh Rivers, locally grown barley and hops, and the best available strains of yeast continue to be the only ingredients in Smithwick's, Ireland's best-selling ale. While at least eight families in Kilkenny were engaged in the business of common or public brewing at the time, it was the Smithwick Brewery that prospered and grew, especially during the lifetime of Edmund Smithwick, for whom the current brewery, E.

Smithwick & Sons, Ltd., is named. Smithwick's golden color and rich flavor offer a delightful alternative to those who prefer drinking ale over stout.

Today, brewing in Ireland is dominated by three large brewing companies: Diageo (Guinness, Smithwick, and Harp, a lager similar to ale or to a European pilsner), Heineken Ireland (Murphy's), and Scottish Newcastle (Beamish & Crawford). As an alternative to mass production, several small, independent breweries have been founded to specialize in the production of stouts, beers, and real ale—cask-conditioned brews that continue to ferment in the barrel or bottle. Hilden Brewing Company in Lisburn, County Antrim; Kinsale Brewing Company in Kinsale, County Cork; the Biddy Early Brewery in Inagh, County Clare; and Carlow Brewing Company in Carlow, County Carlow; produce small batches of unpasteurized ales and stouts, which most drinkers feel have more complexity, flavor, and personality. (See New Brews, pages 55, 61, 62, and 65.)

The special association of food with beer, stout, and ale is a long-standing one in Ireland, especially as an accompaniment to a ploughman's lunch, a platter of oysters, or a slab of beef. Guinness, in fact, calls this relationship "the perfect partnership" and suggests, "Few things in life complement each other as smoothly." I further believe that these affable brews are perfect tenderizers for meat, perfect flavor enhancers for fish, and perfect natural sweeteners in puddings, cakes, pies, and tarts.

Previous spread, top: Fennessy's Hotel and Tavern, Clonmel, County Tipperary.
Previous spread, bottom: Barley and hops are traditional ingredients in Irish brews such as Guinness and Murphys Stout.

LAMB SHANKS BRAISED in STOUT

This recipe is reminiscent of the way French cooks braise meat in red wine. Braising lamb shanks in stout works in much the same way to flavor and tenderize the meat, and adding traditional vegetables like parsnips and a turnip makes it a genuine Irish dish. New Yorker Larry Ryan, an Ireland aficionado and frequent visitor to the Loop Head area of County Clare, created this recipe.

SERVES 6 AS A MAIN COURSE

---

1 cup all-purpose flour

Salt and freshly ground pepper

6 lamb shanks

⅓ cup olive oil

12 small white onions

3 stalks celery, sliced

1 clove garlic, finely chopped

1 cup Irish stout

1 cup homemade beef stock or canned low-sodium beef broth

1 sprig fresh rosemary

1 sprig fresh thyme

12 small potatoes, peeled

1 small turnip, peeled and cut into 1-inch pieces

2 parsnips, peeled and thickly sliced

3 large carrots, peeled and thickly sliced

In a large bowl or resealable plastic bag, combine the flour and salt and pepper to taste. Lightly moisten the lamb shanks with water and dredge them in the flour mixture.

In a large skillet over medium heat, heat the oil. Add the lamb shanks and cook for 8 to 10 minutes, or until browned on all sides. Transfer to a Dutch oven.

Add the onions, celery, and garlic to the skillet and cook for 5 minutes, stirring constantly to scrape up the browned bits from the bottom of the pan. Add the cooked vegetables and pan juices to the lamb in the Dutch oven. Add the stout, stock or broth, rosemary, and thyme. Reduce the heat to low, cover, and simmer for about 1½ hours, or until the lamb is nearly tender. Add the potatoes, turnip, parsnips, and carrots, cover, and cook for 45 to 50 minutes longer, or until the meat and vegetables are tender when pierced with a fork.

To serve, place a lamb shank in the center of each of 6 shallow soup bowls, and spoon the vegetables and broth around them.

MEDIEVAL STEW with STOUT

Beef stew laced with stout is second only to Irish stew as a dish with national identity. It's a favorite pub meal, a perfect do-ahead meal at home (it can be made a day ahead and reheated), and with its mix of traditional ingredients—potatoes, carrots, beef, and stout—it's a real Irish classic. As with all classics, there are many variations, but this recipe from Frankie Sheedy, now chef-proprietor at Ballinalacken Castle, in Doolin, County Clare, has always been my favorite. Serve this with Guinness and Malt Wheaten Bread.

SERVES 6 AS A MAIN COURSE

2 tablespoons canola oil	1 tablespoon raisins
2 pounds lean beef, cut into 1-inch cubes	1 tablespoon tomato purée
3 large onions, sliced	Salt and freshly ground pepper
¼ cup all-purpose flour	8 carrots, peeled and thickly sliced
4 stalks celery, thickly sliced	2 tablespoons minced fresh flat-leaf parsley
8 cups homemade beef stock or canned low-sodium beef broth	Boiled potatoes for serving
1 cup Guinness stout	Guinness and Malt Wheaten Bread (page 60) for serving
1 teaspoon caraway seeds	

In a stockpot or Dutch oven over medium-high heat, heat the oil. Add the meat and cook, stirring constantly, for 5 to 6 minutes, or until browned on all sides. With a slotted spoon, remove the meat and set aside.

Reduce the heat to medium, add the onions, and cook for 3 to 4 minutes, or until soft but not browned. Add the flour and stir to coat the onions. Return the meat to the pot and add the celery, stock or broth, stout, caraway seeds, raisins, tomato purée, and salt and pepper to taste. Cover, reduce the heat to low, and simmer for 2 hours, or until the meat is nearly tender. Add the carrots and cook for 30 to 40 minutes longer, or until the meat and carrots are tender when pierced with a fork.

To serve, ladle the stew into shallow bowls and sprinkle with the parsley. Serve with boiled potatoes and the bread.

MURPHY'S ONION SOUP

The French may have invented onion soup, but it took the Irish to give it a flavor all its own. In this recipe, Murphy's Irish stout gives the traditional soup not only a hearty deep, rich color, but also a unique, malty flavor. Instead of the traditional topping of Gruyére cheese, try it with Kerrygold Swiss or Blarney cheese.

SERVES 8 AS A STARTER

---

2 tablespoons unsalted Kerrygold Irish butter

3 large yellow onions, sliced

2 large red onions, sliced

4 shallots, minced

2 cloves garlic, minced

2 bay leaves

1 teaspoon dried basil

1 teaspoon dried thyme

1 tablespoon dark brown sugar

3 cups homemade beef stock or canned low-sodium beef broth

1 cup Murphy's Irish stout

Salt and freshly ground pepper

1 cup (4 ounces) shredded Kerrygold Swiss or Blarney cheese for topping

---

In a large saucepan over medium heat, melt the butter. Add the onions, shallots, and garlic, and cook for 12 to 15 minutes, or until the onions are soft but not browned. Add the bay leaves, basil, thyme, brown sugar, stock or broth, and stout. Bring to a boil, then reduce the heat to low and simmer, covered, for 25 to 30 minutes, or until the onions are tender. Season to taste with salt and pepper.

Preheat the broiler. Arrange 8 flameproof crocks on a baking sheet. Ladle the soup into the crocks and sprinkle with the cheese. Place under the broiler 4 inches from the heat source and broil for 1 to 2 minutes, or until the cheese melts and starts to brown. Remove from the oven. Using oven mitts to protect your hands, place a crock in the center of each of 8 serving plates, and serve immediately.

BEEF in ALE with CHEESE COBBLER

Hilden Brewing Company in Lisburn, County Antrim, is Ireland's oldest independent brewery. Established in 1982 to reintroduce the tradition of a local brewery making beers of quality and taste, the brewery is housed in nineteenth-century stables. It's open daily for tours and tasting, and its Tap Room restaurant is as popular with locals as it is with visitors. This beef casserole dish, which is served at the restaurant, is made with Scullion's Irish ale, one of three brewed at Hilden. Topped with a cheesy Cheddar cobbler, the dish can be prepared in advance, with the cobbler added just before serving time.

SERVES 4 TO 6 AS A MAIN COURSE

Casserole

2 tablespoons all-purpose flour

Salt and freshly ground pepper

1½ pounds beef brisket, cut into ½-inch-wide strips

2 tablespoons olive oil

1 medium onion, diced

1 clove garlic, minced

2 carrots, peeled and diced

3 stalks celery, diced

2 cups Scullion's Irish ale or similar premium ale

2 cups homemade beef stock or canned low-sodium beef broth

1 tablespoon tomato purée

1 tablespoon Worcestershire sauce

1 sprig fresh thyme

Cobbler

2 cups self-rising flour

½ teaspoon dry mustard

Salt and freshly ground pepper

3 tablespoons cold unsalted Kerrygold Irish butter

1 cup (4 ounces) shredded Kerrygold Vintage Cheddar

½ teaspoon Tabasco sauce

½ to ⅔ cup water

1 tablespoon milk

To make the casserole: In a large bowl or resealable plastic bag, combine the flour and salt and pepper to taste. Dredge the beef in the flour mixture and set aside. Lightly grease a 3-quart casserole dish.

In a large skillet over medium heat, heat the oil. Add the onion and garlic and cook for 2 to 3 minutes, or until soft but not browned. Add the beef and cook for 3 to 5 minutes, or until browned on all sides. Add the carrots and celery and stir to coat. Stir in the ale, stock or broth, tomato purée, Worcestershire sauce, and thyme. Bring to a boil, then reduce the heat to low, cover, and simmer for 30 minutes, or until the meat and vegetables are tender and the sauce starts to thicken. Transfer the mixture to the prepared dish.

To make the cobbler: Preheat the oven to 350°F. Sift the flour and mustard into a food processor. Season with salt and pepper. Add the butter, and pulse 4 to 5 times, or until the mixture resembles coarse crumbs. Add the cheese, Tabasco, and ½ cup water. Process for 8 to 10 seconds, or until a soft dough forms. Add more water, if necessary. Transfer the dough to a floured surface. Roll it out to ½-inch thickness. With a 3-inch round cookie cutter, cut out rounds. Arrange the rounds on top of the meat mixture, overlapping in a decorative pattern. Brush the tops of the cobbler with the milk. Bake for 30 to 35 minutes, or until the top is golden and the mixture is heated through. Remove from the oven and serve immediately.

New Brews: Hilden Brewing Company

The craft of brewing is alive and well at Hilden House, a gracious nineteenth-century Georgian mansion located in the historic village of Lisburn, in County Antrim. Ann and Seamus Scullion established the Hilden Brewing Company in 1982 to reintroduce the tradition of a local brewery making beers of distinctive quality and taste. It is the oldest independent brewery in Ireland. All of their products are made with natural ingredients, are free of additives and preservatives, and use traditional brewing methods, such as bottle and cask conditioning. The Hilden repertoire of distinctive beers includes three brands: Scullion's Irish is a premium live ale that continues to ferment in the bottle. Hilden Original is a bottle-conditioned beer whose freshness and flavor are preserved by a slow secondary fermentation in the bottle. The addition of Golding hops gives the beer a smooth, mellow finish. Molly Malone's is a light stout. The Scullions opened a visitor center in 1996, along with the Tap Room restaurant, which features dishes such as Beef in Ale with Cheese Cobbler.

ALE-BATTERED MUSHROOMS

The medieval city of Kilkenny is home to E. Smithwick & Sons, Ltd., brewers of Smithwick's ale. Many chefs there use the ale in cooking to create lighter-than-air batters for deep-fried mushrooms or shrimp. Serve these mushrooms dipped in Garlic Mayonnaise, Tarragon Mayonnaise, or Honey-Mustard Sauce.

SERVES 4 AS A STARTER

---

²/₃ cup all-purpose flour

1 teaspoon salt

1 teaspoon sugar

2 large eggs

3 tablespoons canola oil, plus additional for frying

1 cup Smithwick's ale

24 large white mushrooms

About 3 cups mixed salad greens

Garlic Mayonnaise, Tarragon Mayonnaise, or Honey-Mustard Sauce (all page 58) for serving

---

In a medium bowl, sift together the flour, salt, and sugar. Make a well in the center. Break the eggs into the well and whisk in the oil and ale. Whisk until a smooth batter forms. Set aside.

Pour enough oil into a large, heavy pot to reach a depth of 3 inches, or fill an electric deep-fryer three-quarters full with oil. Heat until a deep-fat thermometer registers 300°F. Dip the mushrooms into the batter and, working in batches, fry for 3 to 4 minutes per batch, or until the mushrooms are just golden. With a slotted spoon, transfer the mushrooms to paper towels to drain.

To serve, divide the salad greens among 4 serving plates. Place 6 mushrooms on each plate and serve with garlic or tarragon mayonnaise, or honey-mustard sauce.

GARLIC MAYONNAISE

MAKES 1 CUP

> 1 cup mayonnaise
>
> 1 tablespoon minced garlic

In a small bowl, whisk together the mayonnaise and garlic.

TARRAGON MAYONNAISE

MAKES 1 CUP

> 1 cup mayonnaise
>
> 1 tablespoon minced fresh tarragon

In a small bowl, whisk together the mayonnaise and tarragon.

HONEY-MUSTARD SAUCE

MAKES 1 1/2 CUPS

> 1 cup mayonnaise
>
> 3 tablespoons honey
>
> 3 tablespoons Dijon mustard
>
> 1 teaspoon white vinegar
>
> 1 teaspoon ground white pepper

In a small bowl, whisk together the mayonnaise, honey, mustard, vinegar, and pepper. Let stand at room temperature for 10 to 15 minutes to let the flavors meld.

First opened in November 2000, the Guinness Storehouse is based in the heart of the St. James's Gate Brewery, in Dublin, where millions of gallons of Guinness stout are brewed each year. St. James's Gate is the biggest stout brewery in the world.

The building itself was built in 1904, the first steel-framed building in Ireland. Spread out over about four acres of space, the building has as one of its highlights a central glass atrium—cleverly designed in the shape of a pint glass—that opens through seven floors of the entire building. Glass-walled elevators bring visitors on a delightful journey through the past, present, and future of the world's greatest beer, where floor by floor, the ingredients, the process, the time, the craft, and the passion that go into every pint are revealed.

With ten million glasses of Guinness consumed daily in more than 150 countries worldwide (in Ireland, one in two pints consumed is Guinness), it would be hard to find a more perfect place to enjoy a pint than in the Gravity Bar, the end of the tour for visitors to the Storehouse. There you will find an expert barman who gives full attention to the angle at which the glass is held, the speed of the pour, the time given for the pint to settle, and the moment chosen for the top-off—matters of great importance to Guinness drinkers. Located 2.5 meters above the roof level, Gravity Bar is the highest in Dublin. While relaxing with your complimentary pint, you also can enjoy an uninterrupted 360-degree panoramic view of Dublin and its surroundings, from Phoenix Park down the River Liffey and out onto Dublin Bay and the Wicklow Mountains. Since its opening, the Storehouse has hosted two million visitors and is currently the number one visitor attraction in the country (see Resources, page 151).

Traditional Guinness advertising sign.

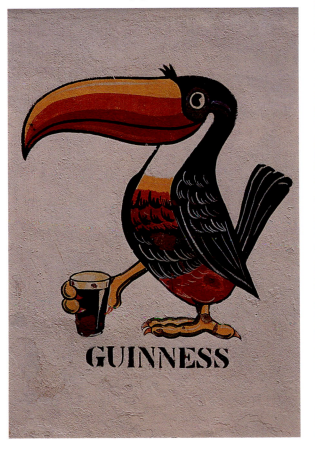

GUINNESS and MALT WHEATEN BREAD

The recipe for this unusual bread comes from Margaret Waterworth, who baked it daily for her guests at Adelboden Country Lodge and Kitchen, in Groomsport, County Down. Mrs. Waterworth and her husband now operate Pier 36, a charming pub in Donaghadee, County Down, where she continues to serve this moist, malty bread.

MAKES 1 LOAF

---

2 cups fine whole-wheat flour, plus additional for sprinkling

2 cups coarse whole-wheat flour or 1 cup each wheat bran and McCann's quick-cooking Irish oatmeal

½ cup sugar

1 teapoon baking soda

1 teaspoon salt

½ cup (1 stick) unsalted Kerrygold Irish butter cut into small pieces

1½ teaspoons barley malt extract (see Note)

1¼ cups buttermilk

1¼ cups Guinness stout

Preheat the oven to 375°F. Grease a 9-by-5-by-3-inch loaf pan and sprinkle with whole-wheat flour.

In a large mixing bowl, combine the flours, sugar, baking soda, and salt. With a pastry cutter or 2 forks, work in the butter until the mixture resembles coarse bread crumbs. Make a well in the center, add the malt, buttermilk, and stout, and mix with a wooden spoon to a porridge consistency. Do not overbeat.

Pour into the prepared pan. Sprinkle additional flour on top and bake for 30 minutes. Reduce the oven temperature to 325°F, and bake for 30 minutes longer. The bread is done when it springs back after being gently pressed on top. Turn the oven off and let the bread cool with the oven door open for 30 minutes. Remove from the oven, remove from the pan, and let it cool on a wire rack before slicing.

Note: Malt extract, also called barley malt, is available in health food stores.

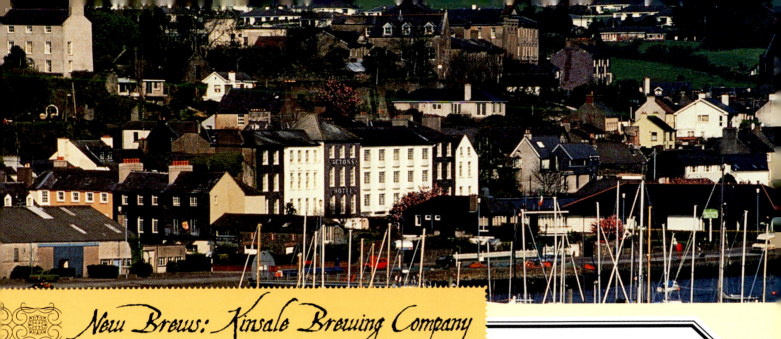

New Brews: Kinsale Brewing Company

Kinsale Brewing Company is a craft brewing facility in Kinsale, County Cork. The Keily brothers, who opened the brewery in September 2001, established it in Kinsale as a tribute to the town's strong brewing tradition, one that dates to the 1700s. Due to its location on the western edge of Europe, Kinsale became the last port of call for many travelers and explorers to the New World. The fusion of these diverse influences has given Kinsale a colorful and cosmopolitan past. Not surprisingly, taverns and brew houses have always been a feature of the town, designed to sustain and entertain the myriad international travelers, traders, mariners, and pirates who crowded the harbor and the town in ages past.

Against this historical backdrop, the Keilys discovered the crumbling remains of Landers Malt House, a three-hundred-year-old brewery, which operated in the center of Kinsale town. They acquired the site in 1997 and began the process of reviving a brewing tradition that had been lost to the town for more than a hundred years. The brewery is open daily for tours and tasting (see Resources, page 151).

Above: View of Kinsale harbor from the nearby village of Scilly, County Cork.

New Brews: Biddy Early Brewery

Ireland is famous for its beer, and in the past, every town in the country had its own brewery. In the late nineteenth century, large companies began edging out the small local breweries, and by the end of the twentieth century, only three large brewing companies remained. In an effort to provide drinkers with an alternative to mass-produced beers, several microbreweries began producing craft beers and ales.

Dr. Peadar Garvey, an industrial chemist who also owned a pub, established the Biddy Early Brewery in 1995 in Inagh, County Clare. He was determined to make small quantities of carefully crafted beers with only natural ingredients. Even though the brew batches remain small, the success of these beers has enabled the brewery to expand, and now the pub-brewery includes a visitor center, where people can get involved in the brewing process. Beers from the Biddy Early Brewery are made with natural ingredients, such as carrageen moss, which is picked in nearby Liscannor Bay, and bog myrtle, which is picked on the mountain at the back of the brewery. Both of these provide a surprisingly fresh flavor.

The brewery produces four beers. Black Biddy is a fruity stout with a rich, malty aroma; a creamy, hoppy palate; and a long, bittersweet finish. Blonde Biddy is a light, pilsner-style lager made with Hallertau hops. The taste is malty, with a hint of fruit. Red Biddy is Ireland's only herb beer, made from bog myrtle, a natural ingredient used to flavor beers before the discovery of hops. It has a slightly sweet taste with overtones of heather. Real Biddy, similar to Red Biddy, is cask conditioned and hand pumped in the traditional style (see Resources, page 151).

BIDDY-BRINED PORK CHOPS

The Biddy Early Brewery, in Inagh, County Clare, is Ireland's first pub-brewery (see facing page). It was established in 1995 to provide drinkers with an alternative to mass-produced beers. They brew five different types of beer, from a hearty stout called Black Biddy to a light, cask-conditioned ale called Real Biddy. The lighter ales are more suitable for the brine in this recipe, a technique that creates a very moist, juicy chop. These chops are delicious with Apple-Pear Chutney and Crushed Potatoes.

SERVES 6 AS A MAIN COURSE

5 cups water	6 allspice berries
½ cup coarse salt	1 bay leaf
½ cup light brown sugar	6 bone-in center-cut pork chops, 1¼ to 1½ inches thick
3 bottles Red Biddy or similar premium ale, or 3 bottles Blonde Biddy or similar European-style pilsner	Apple-Pear Chutney (page 89) for serving
	Crushed Potatoes (page 21) for serving

In a large saucepan over medium heat, bring the water to a boil. Add the salt and brown sugar and cook for 4 to 5 minutes, or until dissolved. Remove from the heat and stir in the ale, allspice, and bay leaf. Let the mixture cool to room temperature. Put the pork chops in a large resealable plastic bag, pour the beer brine in, seal, and refrigerate for 4 to 6 hours. Turn the bag periodically.

Prepare a medium-hot fire in a charcoal grill, or preheat a gas grill to medium-high. Remove the chops from the marinade and pat dry. Grill the pork chops for about 10 minutes on each side, or until an instant-read thermometer inserted into the center of the chops registers 145°F to 150°F. Move the chops to a cooler part of the grill if browning too quickly. Transfer the chops to a platter, cover with foil, and let stand for 5 minutes before serving with the chutney and potatoes.

KILKENNY CHEESE SOUFFLÉS

I'm always on the lookout for new ways to liven up a soufflé, so I often experiment with different varieties of Irish cheese, especially those from the Kerrygold brand (see Note). A friend from Kilkenny suggested this recipe, which uses the locally brewed Smithwick's ale, two varieties of Kerrygold cheese, and zucchini, which the Irish call by their French name, courgettes.

SERVE 6 AS A STARTER

2 medium zucchini (about 1 pound)	Salt and freshly ground pepper
2 tablespoons olive oil	Pinch of cayenne pepper
1 shallot, finely minced	3 large egg yolks
¾ cup milk	¼ cup (1 ounce) shredded Kerrygold Swiss cheese
½ cup Smithwick's ale	¼ cup (1 ounce) grated Dubliner cheese
4 tablespoons unsalted Kerrygold Irish butter	4 large egg whites
½ cup all-purpose flour	

Preheat the oven to 375°F. Generously butter six 8-ounce ramekins.

Using the large holes of a box grater, grate the zucchini into a medium bowl and sprinkle with salt. In a large skillet over medium-low heat, heat the oil. Stir in the shallot and zucchini and cook, stirring frequently, for 18 to 20 minutes, or until very tender. Remove the skillet from the heat and mash the zucchini with a wooden spoon or fork. Set aside.

In a small saucepan over medium heat, bring the milk and ale gently to a boil. Set aside. In a medium saucepan over medium heat, melt the butter. Whisk in the flour and cook for 1 to 2 minutes, or until blended. Slowly whisk in the milk mixture and cook, whisking constantly, for 2 to 3 minutes, or until the mixture is thick and smooth. Season to taste with salt, pepper, and cayenne. Remove from the heat and whisk in the egg yolks, zucchini, and cheeses.

Beat the egg whites with an electric mixer until stiff peaks form. Fold a few tablespoons of the whites into the cheese mixture to lighten it, then gently fold in the remaining whites. Spoon into the prepared ramekins and bake for 20 to 25 minutes, or until the soufflés have risen and the tops are golden. Remove from the oven and serve immediately.

Note: Kerrygold cheeses are made in Ireland from milk supplied by farmers who are members of a dairy cooperative. They make six cheeses: Swiss, Blarney, Smoked Blarney, Dubliner, Vintage Cheddar, and Kerrygold Blue.

New Brews: Carlow Brewing Company

Carlow Brewing Company, a microbrewery founded by the O'Hara brothers in 1996, has revived a tradition that was once synonymous with the Barrow Valley, the traditional heartland of the brewing industry in Ireland. Since its inception, it has established itself as a leading small brewery in Ireland. O'Hara's Celtic Stout won the championship trophy and a gold medal at the Brewing Industry International Awards in April 2000, testifying to the quality and international appeal of its products. The brewery also produces Curim Gold Celtic, a wheat beer, and Molings, a traditional red ale known as O'Hara's Red in the United States.

Barley and hops were once farmed extensively in the Barrow Valley, supported by the many old malting and grain mills that are still prevalent in the landscape. Records show that in the early 1800s, there were five breweries in operation in Carlow. The last of these closed at the end of the nineteenth century. With a dedication to quality reminiscent of bygone brewers, Carlow Brewing Company has grown significantly and now exports beers to a number of countries, including the United Kingdom, the United States, Scandinavia, and continental Europe. The brewery is housed in The Goods Store, a superb old stone building that was originally a provisions center for traders. It is open for tours and tasting by appointment (see Resources, page 151).

The Legend of Biddy Early

Who is Biddy Early, the woman for whom the pub-brewery is named? According to legend (and some lore from the Garvey family, who own it), Biddy O'Connor was born in North Clare in 1798. As a young girl, she was babysitting a neighbor's child when the fairies came and left an *iarlas* (changeling) and took away the human baby. The fairy child grew so fond of Biddy that he gave her a magic bottle that gave her the power to see into the future and cure all sorts of ills. A sip from her bottle was known to cure anything, from infertility in humans to arthritis in animals. This power, of course, landed her in trouble with the Church, and soon she was labeled a witch. When she was twenty, Biddy married a man called Early, and once she was widowed, she married three times more, the last time when she was nearly eighty. Obviously, she didn't let her husbands near the bottle! When Biddy lay dying in 1874, she was persuaded to make her peace with the Church. A priest in Inagh was called to give Biddy the last rites, and legend has it that just before she passed away, she gave the bottle to the priest. When he came to the bridge of Inagh, fearing what might happen to him, he flung the bottle as far as he could.

In 1995, the bottle was found on the riverbank behind the pub, a clear sign to the Garvey family that the legend of Biddy Early should continue in their brews.

Above: Colorful cottages line Galway, Bay, County Galway.

OYSTERS with BACON, CABBAGE, and GUINNESS SABAYON

A lemony sabayon sauce is enhanced with Guinness stout in this Irish interpretation of oysters Rockefeller. Guinness has long been recommended as a perfect accompaniment to oysters, and in this recipe Derry Clarke, chef-owner of L'Ecrivain in Dublin, serves the oysters on top of cabbage instead of spinach, and tops each with a few bits of bacon.

SERVES 4 AS A STARTER

Guinness Sabayon

2 large egg yolks

½ cup Guinness stout

Dash of fresh lemon juice

Salt and freshly ground pepper

1 cup (2 sticks) unsalted Kerrygold Irish butter, melted

4 outer green cabbage leaves, finely shredded

4 slices bacon, chopped

24 oysters in the shell

4 lemon wedges for serving

To make the sabayon: In a double boiler over simmering water, whisk together the egg yolks, stout, lemon juice, and salt and pepper to taste. Whisk for 3 to 5 minutes, or until the sauce begins to thicken. Remove from the heat, and slowly whisk in the melted butter. Keep warm.

Cook the cabbage in salted boiling water for 1 to 2 minutes, or until slightly wilted. Drain and immerse in cold water. Drain again and pat dry. In a small skillet over medium heat, cook the bacon until crisp. Using a slotted spoon, transfer to paper towels to drain.

Preheat the broiler. Shuck the oysters over a small bowl (see Note). Reserve the deeper half of each shell and rinse under cold water. Place the reserved shells on a bed of rock salt in a baking pan. Divide the cabbage among the shells, put an oyster on top of each, and crumble the bacon over the oysters. Spoon some of the sabayon over each. Place under the broiler 4 inches from the heat source and broil for 1 to 2 minutes, or until the sauce starts to brown and is bubbling. Remove from the oven. Using oven mitts to protect your hands, place 6 oysters on each of 4 serving plates. Serve immediately with a wedge of lemon.

Note: To shuck oysters, insert the end of a strong knife between the halves of the shell just behind the hinge or muscle. Cut through the muscle. Lift off the shallow shell. Loosen the oyster from the shell with the point of the knife.

GUINNESS APPLESAUCE CAKE
with LEMON ICING

No one was more surprised than I to learn that desserts could be made with Irish stouts, beers, and ales. Drinking them was a no-brainer, and using them for marinades and for flavoring stews was a great idea, but I thought desserts were another matter. That was before I realized that the sweet flavor produced by yeast and hops could easily translate to cakes, soufflés, breads, and even ice cream! This recipe originated with the brewers of Guinness more than three decades ago.

SERVES 8 TO 10

Cake

1 ¾ cups all-purpose flour

1 teaspoon baking soda

½ teaspoon salt

½ teaspoon ground cloves

1 teaspoon ground cinnamon

1 cup unsweetened applesauce

¾ cup light brown sugar

½ cup vegetable oil

¼ cup Guinness stout

½ cup chopped golden raisins

½ cup chopped dates

½ cup chopped walnuts

Lemon Icing

½ cup (1 stick) unsalted Kerrygold Irish butter, at room temperature

Juice and grated zest of 1 lemon

1 cup confectioners' sugar

Lemon slices for garnish (optional)

To make the cake: Preheat the oven to 350°F. Grease an 8-inch square pan and line it with wax paper.

In a large bowl, sift together the flour, baking soda, salt, cloves, and cinnamon. Set aside.

In a second large bowl, stir together the applesauce, brown sugar, oil, and stout. Mix thoroughly. Add the flour mixture, a little at a time, beating well after each addition. Stir in the raisins, dates, and walnuts.

Spoon the batter into the prepared pan and bake for 40 to 45 minutes, or until a skewer inserted in the center comes out clean. Remove from the oven and cool on a wire rack for 10 minutes. Invert the pan onto a plate, remove the wax paper, and set the cake upright to cool completely.

To make the icing: In a large bowl, combine the butter and lemon zest. Sift the confectioners' sugar into the butter and beat with an electric mixer until smooth and creamy. Stir in enough lemon juice to make the icing soft enough to spread easily. Spread the icing on top of the cake and smooth the surface with an offset spatula or knife dipped in warm water. Decorate the top with lemon slices, if desired.

RASPBERRY SOUFFLÉS

In the 1990s, Gerard Reidy was chef-proprietor at Parliament House, a restaurant located a short distance from the Smithwick Brewery, in Kilkenny City. He served this popular dessert there for many years before relocating to Sligo, where he now operates a restaurant in the rear of Hargadon's Pub.

SERVES 4

½ cup Smithwick's ale

2 tablespoons all-purpose flour

3 tablespoons unsalted Kerrygold Irish butter, at room temperature

¼ cup granulated sugar

3 ounces (½ cup) fresh raspberries

4 large eggs, separated

¼ teaspoon cream of tartar

Confectioners' sugar for dusting

Preheat the oven to 400°F. Lightly butter four 8-ounce ramekins and dust with granulated sugar, tapping out the excess.

In a large saucepan over medium heat, bring the ale to a boil. Whisk in the flour. Reduce the heat to low and simmer for 5 minutes, or until the mixture is smooth. Remove from the heat.

In a medium bowl, beat the butter and granulated sugar with an electric mixer until smooth. Slowly whisk in the ale mixture. Return to the saucepan and boil again, stirring constantly, for 2 minutes, or until slightly thickened. Stir in the raspberries. Remove from the heat and let cool for 8 to 10 minutes. Whisk in the egg yolks.

In a large bowl, beat the egg whites and cream of tartar with an electric mixer until stiff peaks form. Fold one quarter of the egg whites into the raspberry mixture to lighten it, then gently fold in the remaining egg whites. Pour into the prepared ramekins and bake for 18 to 20 minutes, or until the tops are puffed and golden.

Remove from the oven, dust the tops with confectioners' sugar, and serve immediately.

FEATHER GINGERBREAD

Ginger is a favorite spice in Irish baking, and it's the centerpiece of this light-as-air gingerbread, a dark, spicy confection that dates to the Middle Ages. The malty flavor and carbonation of Guinness also add to the feathery, light texture of this cake, which is very popular at Christmastime. Like many old-fashioned gingerbreads, this one, which originated with the brewers of Guinness more than three decades ago, is delicious served with freshly whipped cream.

SERVES 8 TO 10

---

2 cups self-rising flour

1 tablespoon ground ginger

1 tablespoon ground cinnamon

½ teaspoon ground cloves

½ teaspoon ground nutmeg

½ teaspoon baking soda

¾ cup (1½) sticks unsalted
Kerrygold Irish butter

⅔ cup dark brown sugar

1 cup molasses

2 large eggs, beaten

1 cup Guinness stout

½ cup water

Freshly whipped cream for serving (optional)

Preheat the oven to 350°F. Generously butter a 10-inch Bundt pan and dust with flour, knocking out the excess.

In a large bowl, sift together the flour, ginger, cinnamon, cloves, nutmeg, and baking soda. Set aside.

In a large saucepan over medium heat, melt the butter. Stir in the brown sugar and molasses, and cook for 3 to 4 minutes, or until the sugar is dissolved. Whisk in the eggs. Stir in the flour mixture and, with a wooden spoon, beat until smooth.

In a medium saucepan over medium heat, bring the stout and water to a boil. Stir into the batter until smooth. Pour the batter into the prepared pan and bake for 45 to 50 minutes, or until a skewer inserted in the center comes out clean. Remove from the oven and let cool on a rack for about 5 minutes. Invert the cake onto a platter and let it cool for 5 minutes on a wire rack.

To serve, cut the cake into slices and serve warm with whipped cream, if desired.

BLACK and TAN BROWNIES

Historically, the name "black and tan" refers to the much-reviled auxiliary force of English soldiers sent to Ireland after the Easter Rising to suppress the Irish rebels (see page 75). Eventually, a much-loved drink made with half Guinness stout and half Harp lager assumed the name, and now this two-toned brownie gets it, too. Top it with vanilla ice cream or Guinness Ice Cream.

SERVES 8 TO 10

Tan Brownies	Black Brownies
4 tablespoons unsalted Kerrygold Irish butter, at room temperature	5 ounces (5 squares) unsweetened chocolate
1 cup light brown sugar	½ cup (1 stick) unsalted Kerrygold Irish butter
1 large egg	1 cup superfine sugar
½ teaspoon vanilla extract	4 large eggs
¾ cup all-purpose flour	¼ teaspoon salt
1 teaspoon baking powder	1 cup all-purpose flour
¼ teaspoon salt	2 teaspoons vanilla extract
½ cup chopped pecans	1 cup Guinness stout
	Guinness Ice Cream (page 74) for serving

To make the tan brownies: Preheat the oven to 350°F. Butter an 8-inch square pan.

In a medium bowl, beat the butter and brown sugar with an electric mixer until light and fluffy. Beat in the egg and vanilla. With a wooden spoon, stir in the flour, baking powder, salt, and pecans. The batter will be thick. Spoon it into the prepared pan and spread it evenly with a rubber spatula or with dampened fingers.

To make the black brownies: In a medium bowl, melt the chocolate and butter over a bowl of hot water or in the microwave. Stir until smooth. Stir in the superfine sugar, eggs, salt, flour, and vanilla. Whisk in the stout until smooth.

Pour the black brownie mixture over the tan brownie batter and bake for 30 to 35 minutes, or until a skewer inserted in the center comes out almost clean. Remove from the oven and let cool on a wire rack. To serve, cut into squares and serve with vanilla or Guinness ice cream.

GUINNESS ICE CREAM

Grace Neill's is listed in the *Guinness Book of World Records* as the oldest bar in Ireland. It first opened in 1611 as the King's Arms in Donaghadee, County Down, and was renamed in the nineteenth century for its former landlady, a woman who reportedly greeted all visitors to the inn with a welcoming kiss—in between puffs on her clay pipe. Today, guests at Grace Neill's enjoy a more contemporary welcome and some of Northern Ireland's most inventive cuisine, including a Guinness-spiked ice cream, adapted here, which is a wonderful complement to the Black and Tan Brownies (page 72).

SERVES 8 TO 10; MAKES ABOUT 1 QUART

1½ cups Guinness stout	½ teaspoon vanilla extract
1 cup milk	¼ cup dark corn syrup
1½ cups heavy (whipping) cream	4 large egg yolks
½ cup sugar	

In a small saucepan over medium heat, bring the stout to a boil. Remove from the heat and let cool for 20 to 25 minutes.

In a large saucepan over medium heat, bring the milk, cream, sugar, and vanilla to a boil. Remove from the heat and stir in the corn syrup and stout.

In a large bowl, whisk the egg yolks until smooth. Whisk the milk mixture into the egg yolks, then return the mixture to the saucepan and whisk over medium heat for 7 to 8 minutes, or until the mixture thickens. Transfer to a large bowl and let cool for 1 hour. Cover and refrigerate for 2 hours, then stir well and transfer to a 1-quart ice cream maker and process according to the manufacturer's directions. Transfer to a plastic container and freeze for 3 to 4 hours, or until firm. (The ice cream is best if served shortly after making.)

The Black and Tans

In the early 1920s, the Royal Irish Constabulary (RIC), England's police force in Ireland at the time, initiated a massive recruitment effort for men who were willing to "face the rough and dangerous task" of suppressing the Irish rebels. The recruits were mainly unemployed World War I veterans who were willing to work for 10 shillings a day. They served as an occupation army in Ireland whose major role was to make Ireland "hell for rebels to live in." Since there weren't enough RIC uniforms for the new men, they were outfitted in makeshift ones of khaki tunics and dark green trousers, some with civilian hats and black leather belts. These uniforms led to their being called "black and tans," after a famous pack of hounds, and their reputation for cruelty toward the Irish was legendary.

Despite the negative connotation of the name, someone still managed to put the epithet to use by creating a drink made with half Guinness stout and half Harp lager. To make it, half-fill a tall glass or pint glass with Harp. Rest a spoon over the rim of the glass and slowly pour the Guinness over the spoon. The spoon deflects the Guinness and creates a layer of stout (black) on top of the lager (tan). *Sláinte!*

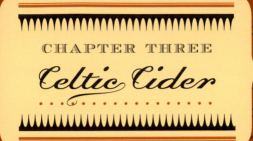

CHAPTER THREE

Celtic Cider

Like so many other natural beverages, cider is one of the most traditional drinks known to man. The process of pressing apples and extracting and fermenting the juice has produced a refreshing alcoholic drink since ancient times. Cider was popular with the ancient Greeks and Romans, and in Christian times, monastic orders were considered to have made an important contribution to the development of orchards for the purpose of cider making. Of all fruits, the apple plays the most important part in legend and folklore, with its hues of green, gold, and russet inspiring tales and traditions that have been passed down through generations of Irish families.

During the Middle Ages, cider was a popular beverage in Ireland, particularly in rural areas. Water supplies in large towns were often unreliable, and tea and coffee were as yet unknown in Europe. As a result, worker and master alike consumed alcoholic beverages, including cider, as the process of brewing produced a safe, bacteria-free drink.

The Anglo-Norman period saw the introduction of orchards in the area of Munster, with this tradition of cultivation later reinforced by English settlers under the "Plantation of Munster." Apple trees were imported from England, along with a group of men skilled in the job of planting new orchards and cultivating the crops to yield a fruitful harvest.

Undoubtedly, Irish cider benefited from the Anglo-Norman influence, and by the seventeenth century, a time known as the First Golden Age of Cider, more than 350 named varieties of cider apples were growing throughout Ireland. Because most farmers could not afford the large outlay of land and slow return from an orchard, most apple orchards were found on large farms and estates. The area around Limerick soon became famous for cider, as did counties Cork, Kerry, and Waterford, and areas in South Tipperary.

Clonmel, in County Tipperary, came to be the home of cider production in Ireland. Situated in a rich and fertile tract of land, Clonmel continues to produce the greater bulk of the best quality of cider apples for the industry. In 1935, a cider-making company began commercial production in Dowd's Lane, where a local man, William Magner, set up his own business. In 1937, he amalgamated with H. P. Bulmer (now a British company), from whose name the famous Bulmers label is derived. Ownership of the label in Ireland is now with the C&C Group PLC, based in Clonmel, a company that maintains the natural and traditional fermentation process, which is important even in modern production.

Today, Bulmers Ltd. produces a wide range of ciders to satisfy a variety of tastes. The most popular in Ireland is Bulmers Original, a traditional medium-sweet vintage cider with a rich, golden color. Strongbow is a medium-dry cider, higher in alcohol than Bulmers but lighter in color. Linden Village contains the same alcohol level as Strongbow, but is less dry in flavor and darker in color. For celebratory purposes, three sparkling ciders are also produced: Vervier, Michelle, and Palais D'Or. Bulmers' export brand, which is what you'll find in the United States, is called Magners Irish Cider.

In Ireland, cider has emerged as a sophisticated drink that many consumers regard as a natural alternative to wine. The two, in fact, undergo the same fermentation process, can be served in similar situations, and can be drunk with equal enjoyment. For years cider has been a popular ingredient in many cuisines, and it is a particular favorite among the Celts, Bretons, and Normans.

Today, home cooks and chefs alike consider cider to be as desirable and flavorsome as wine in a wide range of recipes, especially in sauces for main courses and desserts. Steeping a ham in cider, particularly at Christmastime, is a much-loved tradition, but cooks need not wait for a holiday to experiment with the number of different styles of cider—sweet, medium, dry, sparkling, and still.

Previous spread, top: Rolling hills and valleys of West Cork
Previous spread, bottom: St. Patrick's Day Parade, Dublin

Below: Barley is a key ingredient in making whiskey and stout.

TOMATO-BASIL SOUP

Georgina Campbell is one of Ireland's most respected food writers. The author of the highly acclaimed annual *Guide to the Best Places to Eat, Drink, and Stay in Ireland*, she devised several cider-based recipes for the Cider Industry Council. This tomato and basil soup, which is ideal for a summer meal when tomatoes and basil are at their best, is also flavorful when made with canned tomatoes for an all-season soup. Serve it with Brown Soda Bread generously spread with Kerrygold Irish butter.

SERVES 8 TO 10 AS A STARTER

---

4 tablespoons unsalted Kerrygold Irish butter

2 tablespoons olive oil

1 large onion, finely chopped

1 large stalk celery, finely chopped

2 large carrots, peeled and chopped

1 pound tomatoes, chopped, juices reserved, or one 28-ounce can crushed tomatoes, drained, juices reserved

½ cup tomato purée

1 tablespoon minced garlic

1 bay leaf

2 tablespoons minced fresh basil

4 cups homemade chicken stock or low-sodium canned chicken broth

1½ cups Irish cider

1 tablespoon grated lemon zest

Salt and freshly ground pepper

Crème fraîche for serving (see Note)

Fresh basil leaves for garnish

2 tablespoons minced fresh flat-leaf parsley

Brown Soda Bread (facing page) for serving

In a stockpot or large saucepan over medium heat, melt the butter with the oil. Add the onion, celery, and carrots and cook for 3 to 5 minutes, or until soft but not browned. Stir in the tomatoes, tomato purée, garlic, bay leaf, and basil. Bring to a boil, then reduce the heat to low and stir in the stock or broth, cider, reserved tomato juice, lemon zest, and salt and pepper to taste. Simmer uncovered for 30 minutes, then remove from the heat and let cool for 20 minutes. Remove the bay leaf.

Working in batches, transfer the soup to a food processor or blender and purée until smooth. (Or purée in the pot with an immersion blender.) Return the soup to the pot to heat through.

To serve, ladle the soup into shallow bowls, place a spoonful of crème fraîche in the center of each, and top with a basil leaf. Sprinkle with the parsley and serve with brown bread.

Note: To make crème fraîche, combine 1 cup heavy (whipping) cream with 1 tablespoon buttermilk in a glass jar. Stir to blend, then cover and let stand at room temperature for 12 to 24 hours, or until thickened. Refrigerate.

BROWN SODA BREAD

Every Irish cook has a favorite soda bread recipe and preference for the shape of the loaf. I like this one, which makes two small loaves—one for eating now and one for freezing to later make bread crumbs for cobblers, crisps, and Brown Bread Ice Cream (see page 137).

MAKES 2 SMALL LOAVES

2 ¼ cups all-purpose flour

2 teaspoons baking soda

1 teaspoon baking powder

½ teaspoon salt

2 cups whole-wheat flour

1 cup plus 1 tablespoon McCann's quick-cooking (not instant) Irish oatmeal

2 ¼ cups buttermilk

1 large egg, lightly beaten

Preheat the oven to 325°F. Grease a baking sheet.

In a large bowl, sift together the all-purpose flour, baking soda, baking powder, and salt. Stir in the whole-wheat flour and 1 cup of the oats. Make a well in the center and pour in the buttermilk and egg. With a wooden spoon, stir until the mixture forms a soft dough. With floured hands, form the dough into 2 rounds. Transfer to the prepared baking sheet and sprinkle with the remaining 1 tablespoon oatmeal. Bake for 35 to 40 minutes, or until a skewer inserted in the center comes out clean and the tops are browned. Remove from the oven and let the loaves cool on a wire rack.

PUMPKIN-CIDER SOUP

This hearty autumnal soup pairs two of the season's favorite ingredients, pumpkin and apples, although Hubbard or butternut squash can easily serve as a substitute for the pumpkin. The cider adds a pleasant sweetness.

SERVES 8 TO 10 AS A STARTER

5 tablespoons unsalted Kerrygold Irish butter

2 medium onions, chopped

1 stalk celery, chopped

6 cups (1-inch cubes) pumpkin, Hubbard squash, or butternut squash

2 small Granny Smith apples, peeled, cored, and chopped

5 cups homemade chicken stock or low-sodium canned chicken broth

1 cup Irish cider

2 or 3 fresh sage leaves

1 cup heavy (whipping) cream

Salt and freshly ground pepper

Crème fraîche for serving (see Note, page 80)

Minced fresh flat-leaf parsley for garnish

Chopped fresh chives for garnish

Brown Soda Bread (page 81) for serving

In a stockpot or large saucepan over medium heat, melt the butter. Add the onions and celery, and cook for 3 to 5 minutes, or until soft but not browned. Add the pumpkin or squash, apples, stock or broth, cider, and sage, and bring to a boil. Reduce the heat to low and simmer uncovered, stirring occasionally, for 30 to 40 minutes, or until the vegetables are tender. Remove from the heat and let cool for 10 minutes. Remove the sage leaves.

Working in batches, transfer the soup to a food processor or blender and purée until smooth. (Or purée in the pot with an immersion blender.) Return the soup to the pot, stir in the cream, and cook until heated through. Season to taste with salt and pepper.

To serve, ladle the soup into shallow bowls, place a spoonful of crème fraîche in the center of each, and sprinkle with the parsley and chives. Serve with the brown bread.

CHICKEN with BACON, CABBAGE, and CIDER

Chicken boiled or braised with ham or bacon is a popular Irish dish, and when cabbage is added, it's a complete meal. As a tribute to tradition, this recipe teams up breast of chicken with the time-honored combination of bacon and cabbage, but adds a bit of cider to create a flavorful sauce. Serve this with Boiled New Potatoes.

SERVES 4 AS A MAIN COURSE

4 boneless, skinless chicken breast halves, 5 to 6 ounces each	2 tablespoons minced garlic
Salt and freshly ground pepper	½ cup homemade chicken stock or canned low-sodium chicken broth
6 slices bacon, cut into ¼-inch strips	¾ cup Irish cider
¼ cup canola oil	2 cups shredded savoy cabbage
2 onions, sliced	Boiled New Potatoes (page 21) for serving

Place the chicken breasts between 2 sheets of wax paper and, with a mallet or rolling pin, pound or roll to ½-inch thickness. Season with salt and pepper.

In a large skillet over medium heat, cook the bacon for 5 to 7 minutes, or until crisp. Remove to paper towels to drain. Return the skillet to the stove and heat 2 tablespoons of the oil. Add the chicken and cook for 4 to 5 minutes on each side, or until no longer pink in the center. Remove the chicken from the pan and cover with aluminum foil (the chicken will continue to cook).

In the same skillet over medium heat, heat the remaining 2 tablespoons oil. Stir in the onions and garlic and cook, scraping up the browned bits from the bottom of the pan, for 3 to 5 minutes, or until the vegetables are soft but not browned. Stir in the stock or broth and the cider. Bring to a boil, then add the cabbage. Reduce the heat to medium, cover, and cook for 8 to 10 minutes, or until the cabbage is tender.

With a slotted spoon, transfer the cabbage to a platter and cover with aluminum foil. Boil the cooking liquid for 4 to 5 minutes, or until reduced by half.

To serve, divide the cabbage among 4 serving plates. Slice the chicken and place on top of the cabbage. Spoon the sauce over the top, sprinkle with the reserved bacon, and serve with the potatoes.

PORK TENDERLOIN
with APPLE CIDER SAUCE

The combination of pork and apples is popular in many cuisines, and you'll find dishes featuring them in many Irish homes, restaurants, and pubs. Pork tenderloin, which is very lean and exceptionally versatile, gets added apple flavor power from a light-but-dry Irish cider. If you like, serve this with Buttermilk-Chive Mashed Potatoes.

SERVES 4 AS A MAIN COURSE

---

2 pork tenderloins, 12 ounces each

Salt and freshly ground pepper

4 tablespoons unsalted Kerrygold Irish butter

2 Granny Smith apples, peeled, cored, and quartered

2 tablespoons minced shallot

½ teaspoon crumbled dried sage

½ cup Irish cider

½ cup cider vinegar

1 cup homemade chicken stock or canned low-sodium chicken broth

⅔ cup heavy (whipping) cream

1 tablespoon minced fresh flat-leaf parsley

Buttermilk-Chive Mashed Potatoes (page 20) for serving (optional)

Cut the pork into 1-inch-thick slices. Place the slices between sheets of wax paper and, with a mallet or rolling pin, pound or roll to ¼-inch thickness. Season with salt and pepper.

In a large skillet over medium heat, melt 2 tablespoons of the butter. Add the pork slices and cook for 2 minutes on each side, or until cooked through. Transfer to a warmed platter and cover with aluminum foil.

In the same skillet over medium heat, melt the remaining 2 tablespoons butter. Add the apples and sauté for 2 to 3 minutes, or until the apples are lightly browned. With a slotted spoon, transfer the apples to the platter with the pork.

In the same skillet over medium heat, add the shallot and cook for 1 minute. Add the sage, cider, and vinegar and bring to a boil, scraping up the browned bits from the bottom of the pan. Add the chicken stock or broth and boil, stirring constantly, for 3 to 4 minutes, or until reduced by half. Stir in the cream, pork, and juices from the platter. Cook, turning the pork once or twice, for 1 to 2 minutes, or until the sauce thickens.

To serve, divide the pork slices among 4 serving plates, spoon the sauce over the meat, arrange the apple slices around it, and sprinkle with parsley. Serve with the mashed potatoes, if desired.

GOAT CHEESE and APPLE SALAD with CIDER VINAIGRETTE

One of my favorite Irish cheeses is St. Tola goat cheese, which is made from organic raw goat's milk at Inagh Farmhouse, just south of the rocky Burren area near Ennis, County Clare. This lovely cheese, which Siobhán Ni Gháirbhith makes into logs and individual crottins, has a fresh floral flavor and is delicious in salads. A cider-based vinaigrette flavored with a hint of sage nicely complements its delicate texture and taste. Try serving this salad with Brown Soda Bread (page 81).

SERVES 6 AS A STARTER

Cider Vinaigrette	Salad
½ cup olive oil	About 5 cups mixed salad greens
⅓ cup Irish cider	2 to 3 ounces radicchio or red-leaf lettuce, roughly torn
⅛ teaspoon dried sage	4 ounces goat cheese, preferably Irish, cut into small pieces
1 teaspoon sugar	¼ cup dried cranberries
Salt and freshly ground pepper	3 Granny Smith apples, peeled, cored, and sliced

To make the vinaigrette: Combine all the ingredients in a sealable jar and shake to blend. Set aside.

To make the salad: In a large salad bowl, combine the salad greens and radicchio or red-leaf lettuce. Divide the greens among 6 salad plates and sprinkle with the goat cheese and dried cranberries. Place the apples on top and drizzle with the vinaigrette.

IRISH APPLE-POTATO CAKES

Potato cakes—especially boxty, which is made with grated raw and cooked mashed potatoes—make a great side dish for fish and meat. These unusual ones originated at the Blue Haven Restaurant in Kinsale, County Cork, where the chef originally served them with wild rabbit stew. They're also delicious with scallops.

MAKES 8 CAKES

---

1 pound baking potatoes, peeled and quartered

2 Granny Smith apples, peeled, cored, and sliced

2 tablespoons water

4 tablespoons unsalted Kerrygold Irish butter

¼ cup minced fresh flat-leaf parsley

1 tablespoon all-purpose flour

Salt and freshly ground pepper

2 tablespoons canola oil

Cook the potatoes in boiling salted water for 12 to 15 minutes, or until tender. Drain and mash. In a medium saucepan over medium heat, combine the apples and water. Cook for 8 to 10 minutes, or until the apples begin to break up and are pulpy. Drain the apples and stir into the potatoes. Add 2 tablespoons of the butter, the parsley, flour and salt and pepper to taste. Mix well. With floured hands, form the mixture into 8 flat cakes. Refrigerate for 15 minutes.

In a large skillet over medium heat, heat the remaining 2 tablespoons butter and the oil. Fry the potato cakes for 2 to 3 minutes on each side, or until browned and crisp.

APPLE-PEAR CHUTNEY

This versatile chutney is a great accompaniment to a baked ham, but it's also a lively addition to a cheese board or a ploughman's lunch, a plate of cold meats and cheese. To make a delicious sandwich spread, combine 1 tablespoon of this chutney with 1 tablespoon of Dijon mustard.

MAKES 1¹/₂ CUPS

¹/₃ cup chopped onion	³/₄ cup golden raisins
¹/₃ cup cider vinegar	1¹/₂ cups diced apples
1 teaspoon minced, peeled fresh ginger	1¹/₂ cups diced pears
1 cup packed brown sugar	¹/₄ cup chopped walnuts

In a large, nonreactive saucepan, combine all the ingredients except the walnuts. Bring to a boil, then reduce the heat to medium-low and cook, uncovered, for 20 to 25 minutes, or until thickened. Remove from the heat and stir in the walnuts. Let cool to room temperature. Cover and refrigerate for up to 2 weeks. Return to room temperature before serving.

CIDER-GLAZED SCALLOPS

Cider and seafood may seem an unlikely combination, but they complement each another surprisingly well. This recipe, adapted from a dish served at a Belfast restaurant, pairs scallops with both cider and apples for a light but satisfying dish. Serve with Irish Apple-Potato Cakes.

SERVES 4 AS A MAIN COURSE

1 cup Irish cider	¼ cup minced fresh sage
½ cup dry white wine	2 tablespoons fresh lemon juice
1 pound sea scallops, rinsed and patted dry	1 small Granny Smith apple, unpeeled, cored, sliced, and cut into ¼-inch pieces
Salt and freshly ground pepper	
6 tablespoons unsalted Kerrygold Irish butter	Irish Apple-Potato Cakes (page 88) for serving

In a small saucepan, bring the cider and wine to a boil. Cook, stirring frequently, for 10 to 12 minutes, or until the mixture is reduced to about ¼ cup. Set aside.

Season the scallops with salt and pepper. In a large skillet over medium-high heat, melt 2 tablespoons of the butter. When the butter starts to brown, add the scallops and cook for 2 minutes on each side, or until browned. Remove from the heat, transfer to 2 serving plates, and cover to keep warm.

Return the skillet to the stovetop over medium heat. Melt the remaining 4 tablespoons butter. Stir in the cider mixture, sage, and lemon juice. Bring to a boil, then stir in the apple. Cook for 2 to 3 minutes, or until the sauce thickens and the apple pieces are slightly tender. Season again with salt and pepper. Uncover the scallops and spoon the sauce over the top. Serve with the potato cakes.

CIDER-GLAZED BAKED HAM

Irish people love bacon in any shape or form, and when they eat ham, it's a cut of the pig that's taken from the leg. It's called gammon, or baked ham, and is usually basted in some sweet-tart liquid like cider. Not only is a baked ham great on the day it's served, but leftover ham is also a wonderful ingredient in casseroles and sandwiches. Serve the ham with Apple-Pear Chutney and Rutabaga Purée.

SERVES 12 AS A MAIN COURSE

1 butt half, bone-in, fully cooked ham, 6 to 8 pounds	2 tablespoons dark brown sugar
12 to 15 whole cloves	1 tablespoon Dijon mustard
2 cups Irish cider	Apple-Pear Chutney (page 89) for serving
¼ cup pineapple juice	Rutabaga Purée (page 113) for serving

Preheat the oven to 325°F. Score the ham in a diamond pattern and stud with the cloves. In a small bowl, combine the cider and pineapple juice. Place the ham, cut side down, on a rack in a large roasting pan. Pour the cider mixture over the top. Loosely cover the ham with aluminum foil, and bake for 1½ hours.

Remove the ham from the oven. In a small bowl, combine the brown sugar and mustard. Mix 3 to 4 tablespoons of the cooking liquid with the mustard mixture and spoon it over the ham. Continue to cook, uncovered, basting frequently, for 30 to 40 minutes, or until an instant-read thermometer registers 160°F when inserted into the thickest part of the ham.

Remove the ham to a platter or cutting board. Cover with foil and let stand for 10 to 15 minutes or longer before slicing. Serve with the Apple-Pear Chutney and Rutabaga Purée.

CIDER PUDDING

This "pudding," which is somewhat of a generic term for Irish desserts, is actually a dense sponge cake that gets soaked in cider syrup, similar to mulled wine. For best absorption, it should be made in a shallow, 8- or 9-cup crown-shaped kugelhopf mold, or fluted ring mold.

SERVES 6

Pudding

4 large eggs, separated

¾ cup sugar

Grated zest of ½ lemon

1¼ cups fresh bread crumbs, plus additional for coating pan (see Note, page 25)

Cider Syrup

¾ cup Irish cider

½ cup sugar

2 tablespoons fresh lemon juice

2 tablespoons fresh orange juice

1 cinnamon stick

2 whole cloves

Zest of ½ orange, cut into strips

2 tablespoons whiskey and honey-based liqueur such as Irish Mist, Celtic Crossing, or Eblana (see page 105)

1 cup crème fraîche (see Note, page 80) for serving

Confectioners' sugar for dusting

To make the pudding: Preheat the oven to 350°F. Butter a ring-shaped mold or small Bundt pan and dust with bread crumbs, tapping out the excess.

In a large bowl, beat the egg yolks and ¼ cup of the sugar with an electric mixer until light and fluffy. Stir in the lemon zest and set aside.

In a medium bowl, beat the egg whites with an electric mixer until stiff peaks form. Gradually beat in the remaining ½ cup sugar. Stir one-fourth of the egg-white mixture into the yolks to lighten. Fold in the bread crumbs, then gently fold in the remaining egg whites. Spoon into the prepared pan and bake for 30 to 35 minutes, or until a skewer inserted in the center comes out clean and the top is golden. Remove from the oven and let cool on a wire rack for 5 minutes.

To make the syrup: In a medium saucepan over medium heat, combine the cider, sugar, lemon juice, orange juice, cinnamon, and cloves. Bring to a boil, then remove from the heat and stir in the orange zest and liqueur. Let cool for 30 minutes, then strain into a small bowl, and cool completely.

Invert the pudding onto a shallow dish and spoon one-third of the syrup over the top. Let the syrup soak in, then continue to spoon the syrup over the cake until it has all been absorbed. Cover and refrigerate for 2 to 3 hours.

To serve, remove the cake from the refrigerator and cut it into slices. Serve with a spoonful of crème fraîche and a dusting of confectioners' sugar.

Rock of Cashel, Cashel, County Tipperary

APPLE CAKE with TOFFEE SAUCE

This three-part dessert, from a collection of cider-influenced recipes from Belfast chefs Jeanne and Paul Rankin, starts with roasted apples and ends with a luscious caramel cream topping. In between is a chunky, old-fashioned apple-butter cake, one of the most popular cakes in Irish cookery.

SERVES 8 TO 10

Roasted Apples

8 Granny Smith apples, peeled, cored, and quartered

Juice of 2 lemons

⅔ cup sugar

4 tablespoons unsalted Kerrygold Irish butter

Cake

½ cup slivered almonds

1½ cups all-purpose flour

1 teaspoon ground cinnamon

1 teaspoon baking soda

Pinch of salt

½ cup (1 stick) unsalted Kerrygold Irish butter, at room temperature

1 cup sugar

3 large eggs

1 teaspoon vanilla extract

½ cup sour cream or crème fraîche (see Note, page 80)

¼ cup Irish cider

Toffee Sauce

¾ cup water

¾ cup sugar

1 tablespoon fresh lemon juice

¾ cup heavy (whipping) cream

To make the roasted apples: Preheat the oven to 375°F. Butter a large casserole dish. Cut the apple quarters into 2 to 3 wedges each and place in the prepared dish. Sprinkle with the lemon juice and sugar, and dot with the butter. Bake, turning frequently, for 15 to 20 minutes, or until the apples are tender when pierced with the tip of a knife. Remove from the oven, drain off the juices, and set the apples aside to cool. Maintain the oven temperature.

To make the cake: Butter a 9- or 10-inch springform pan and sprinkle the bottom with the almonds.

In a medium bowl, sift together the flour, cinnamon, baking soda, and salt. Set aside. In a large bowl, cream the butter and sugar with an electric mixer until light and fluffy. Add the eggs, one at a time, and continue to beat until the mixture is smooth. With a wooden spoon, fold in the dry ingredients, the vanilla, sour cream or crème fraîche, and cider.

CONTINUED

APPLE CAKE with TOFFEE SAUCE continued

Starting in the center, decoratively arrange half of the apples in the bottom of the prepared pan. Roughly chop the remaining apples and stir into the cake batter. Pour the batter into the pan and bake for 70 to 80 minutes, or until a skewer inserted in the center comes out clean. Remove the cake from the oven and let cool on a wire rack for 10 minutes. Release the sides of the pan, invert the cake onto a plate, and remove the base.

To make the toffee sauce: In a medium saucepan, bring the water and sugar to a boil. Stir in the lemon juice. Cook for 10 to 15 minutes, or until the mixture begins to turn a light caramel color. Remove from the heat and slowly whisk in the cream.

To serve, cut the cake into slices and drizzle with the toffee sauce.

CREAM CHEESE POUND CAKE with CIDER-CREAM SAUCE

The name "pound cake" comes from the rather precise recipe for a cake that calls for 1 pound of sugar, 1 pound of butter, and 1 pound of flour. Some additional flavoring, such as nutmeg, lemon juice, or vanilla, is often added. Today the ratio of sugar to butter to flour sometimes varies, but the results are usually the same. Pound cake is one of those reliable cakes that every culture seems to embrace because it goes well with everything—fresh fruit, fruit compote, ice cream, sabayon, and creamy sauces like this one made with Irish cider. The cream cheese in this recipe, which comes from a baker friend in County Galway, is a pleasant addition.

SERVES 12

Cake

1 cup (2 sticks) unsalted Kerrygold Irish butter, at room temperature

One 8-ounce package cream cheese, at room temperature

2 cups sugar

2 teaspoons vanilla extract

2 1/3 cups self-rising cake flour

6 large eggs, at room temperature

Cider-Cream Sauce

3 cups Irish cider

1 cup heavy (whipping) cream

2 tablespoons unsalted Kerrygold Irish butter, cut into small pieces

1/4 teaspoon vanilla extract

1 teaspoon fresh lemon juice

To make the cake: Preheat the oven to 350°F. Butter a 10-inch round tube pan and line with parchment paper.

In the large bowl of a stand mixer, beat the butter and cream cheese for 5 minutes, or until light and fluffy. Add the sugar, vanilla, and flour and beat on medium-low speed for 2 to 3 minutes, or until well combined. Add the eggs, one at a time, beating well after each addition and scraping down the sides of the bowl, if necessary.

CONTINUED

CREAM CHEESE POUND CAKE with CIDER-CREAM SAUCE continued

Pour the batter into the prepared pan, smooth the top with a spatula, and tap the pan to remove any air bubbles. Bake for about 50 minutes, or until a skewer inserted in the center comes out clean. Remove the cake from the oven and let it cool on a wire rack for 15 minutes. Invert the pan onto a plate, remove the pan, then return the cake to upright and let cool completely.

To make the sauce: In a medium saucepan, bring the cider to a boil. Cook for 15 to 18 minutes, or until reduced to about ½ cup. Whisk in the cream and cook for 2 to 3 minutes, or until thickened. Remove from the heat and whisk in the butter, vanilla, and lemon juice. Cool completely, then refrigerate for 1 hour or more, or until cold.

To serve, cut the cake into slices and spoon the cider sauce over the top.

FRUITY SPONGE CAKE
with CIDER SABAYON

The Cider Industry Council, based in Dublin, is dedicated to all facets of cider production and promotion, including campaigns for responsible drinking. They also regularly invite chefs to devise recipes using cider, and several times a year they publish these recipes for home cooks. This sponge cake, from well-known cookery writer Biddy White Lennon, is traditionally made with apples and served at Halloween, but she substitutes pears. She suggests you serve it warm with the cider sabayon, or cold with whipped cream.

SERVES 8 TO 10

Cake	Cider Sabayon
2 cups self-rising flour	4 large egg yolks
1 teaspoon baking soda	¾ cup sugar
½ teaspoon ground nutmeg	1 cup Irish cider
½ cup (1 stick) unsalted Kerrygold Irish butter, at room temperature	
½ cup sugar	Fresh raspberries for garnish
2 large eggs, beaten	Fresh mint leaves for garnish
1 cup Irish cider	
2 to 3 Bartlett or Anjou pears, peeled, cored, and cut into thin slices	

To make the cake: Preheat the oven to 350°F. Butter an 8- or 9-inch square nonstick baking pan.

In a medium bowl, sift together the flour, baking soda, and nutmeg. Set aside. In a large bowl, beat the butter and sugar with an electric mixer until light and fluffy. Beat in 1 cup of the flour mixture and the eggs, then beat in the cider and the remaining flour mixture until smooth. Pour the batter into the prepared pan and lightly press the pear slices in rows, core side down, into the batter. Bake for 30 to 35 minutes, or until a skewer inserted in the center comes out clean. Remove from the oven and let cool on a wire rack.

To make the sabayon: In a double boiler or large stainless steel bowl set over simmering water, whisk together the egg yolks and sugar. Whisk for 8 to 10 minutes, or until the mixture thickens. Add the cider, and continue to whisk until the mixture is smooth. Remove from the heat.

To serve, cut the cake into squares and spoon the sauce over the top. Garnish with fresh raspberries and mint leaves.

Of all the world's alcoholic beverages, wine is the oldest. Archaeologists maintain that grape wine, or something like it, was made at least ten thousand years ago, with mention of wine as "a gift from the gods" found in Egyptian, Greek, and Roman histories. Ancient scholars tell of Noah's planting a vineyard near Erivan, and the Old Testament mentions wine more than 150 times. According to some sources, grape seeds have been found in prehistoric caves.

But even before the advent of grape wine, honey was fermented with water and herbs to create a beverage known as mead. As early as the fifth century, this honey-based wine was a popular drink of Anglo, Saxon, and Jute warriors, although secretive Irish monks, who fermented their excess honey with water, grape juice, and herbs, were already producing it.

Eventually, mead came to be the chief drink of the Irish and is often mentioned in Gaelic poetry. Its influence was so great that the halls of Tara, where the high kings of Ireland ruled, was called the House of the Mead Circle. Its fame as a refreshing drink spread quickly throughout Ireland, and soon no medieval banquet was complete without mead to accompany it. This honey wine was also believed to have powers of virility and fertility, and it became the custom at weddings for the bride and groom to be toasted with special goblets full of mead, which they would use for one full moon after the wedding. This tradition is the origin of the word "honeymoon" (see page 123).

But with the tumult of the Middle Ages, the monks' secret method of making mead was lost to the Irish for more than five hundred years. It wasn't until recently that the recipe for mead was rediscovered. Today, mead is once again being produced in Ireland at the Bunratty Winery, an old coach house situated in the shadow of the now-famous Bunratty Castle in County Clare. This ancient drink, always regarded as one "fit for a king," has been reinvented for the modern world, to be drunk as an aperitif or table wine. It's also the mainstay at Ireland's popular medieval castle banquets. Bunratty Mead is equally pleasant as an ingredient in cooking. Its mellow taste adds a subtle sweetness to meats, poultry, and vegetables and, like other fine wines used in cooking, it can be the basis of an exciting and elegant meal, one even "fit for a king."

Another drink favored by the chieftains and nobles of Ireland's ancient clans was one called heather wine, which was actually a spirit flavored with honey, herbs, and spices. The secret of this legendary drink also disappeared for centuries with the great exodus of the Irish earls in 1691, an event that has passed into Irish history as "the flight of the wild geese." The recipe was thought to have been lost forever until some European travelers visiting Ireland in the 1940s produced an old manuscript they had found. Daniel E. Williams, whose family founded the Tullamore Distillery, recognized it as the ancient recipe and transformed it into what is now Irish Mist liqueur.

Inherent in the transformation was Williams's devotion to the authenticity and originality of Ireland's legendary liqueur—the blending of great distilled spirits, the mellowing and maturing process, and the mingling of Irish honeys and exotic herbs. This alone could create the luxurious taste of Irish Mist, one of Ireland's most treasured libations. Yet as treasured and exceptional as Irish Mist is, it remains a drink for all occasions—neat or with ice or soda. Its perfect balance of potency, good taste, and bouquet makes it an extraordinary ingredient in food as well, complementing meats and fish and adding incomparable flavor to desserts.

Like Irish Mist, Celtic Crossing—a blend of Irish whiskeys, Cognac, and honey—is making its mark on the drinking and cooking worlds. Launched in 1996 by Castle Brands, it was created to commemorate the 150th anniversary of the Irish famine and to remember all those who had to leave Ireland to seek new lives elsewhere. The newest addition to this range of spirits is Eblana, an ancient name for Dublin, with flavors of toasted almonds, caramel, and coffee. Eblana, from the makers of Cooley whiskey, debuted in 1999.

Previous spread, top: Dunguaire Castle, Kinvara, County Galway
Previous spread, bottom: Crystal waters from mountain streams contribute to the purity of Irish drinks.

DUBLIN BAY SHRIMP TOAST

This cream cheese spread is perfect party fare. You can make it ahead of time and spread it on the bread just before serving. The Irish Mist liqueur adds a touch of sweetness. The recipe can easily be doubled.

MAKES 20 TO 25 TOASTS

One 8-ounce package cream cheese, at room temperature

One 4-ounce can shrimp, rinsed and drained

¼ cup mayonnaise

2 tablespoons Irish Mist liqueur

1 tablespoon fresh lemon juice

1 tablespoon minced fresh flat-leaf parsley

Salt and freshly ground pepper

One 1-pound package cocktail rye bread

20 to 25 small shrimp, cooked and peeled

Preheat the broiler.

In a medium bowl, combine the cream cheese, canned shrimp, mayonnaise, Irish Mist, lemon juice, parsley, and salt and pepper to taste. Stir until smooth.

Arrange the slices of bread on a baking sheet and toast under the broiler, 4 inches from the heat source, for 2 minutes on each side, or until lightly toasted. Spread one side of each slice with the shrimp mixture, and return to the broiler for 1 minute, or until the mixture bubbles and browns. Remove from the broiler and put 1 whole cooked shrimp on top of each. Serve immediately.

IRISH FONDUE

Fondue is fashionable once again, and this recipe offers an Irish version of the traditional Swiss dish, pairing the honey wine known as mead with three of the delicious cheeses from the Kerrygold range. Unlike the standard fondue, in which the cheese is melted in a pot and cubes of bread are dipped into it, here the cheese is baked into the bread and served in finger-size strips or bite-size squares. It's a perfect Irish hors d'oeuvres.

MAKES ABOUT 48 PIECES

½ cup (1 stick) unsalted Kerrygold Irish butter or Kerrygold Garlic and Herb Butter, at room temperature (see Note)

½ teaspoon dry mustard

½ teaspoon minced garlic

¼ teaspoon chopped chives

Salt and freshly ground pepper

16 slices firm-textured white bread, such as Pepperidge Farm brand, crusts removed

1 cup (4 ounces) shredded Kerrygold Blarney cheese

1 cup (4 ounces) shredded Kerrygold Swiss cheese

4 large eggs

1 cup milk

⅔ cup Bunratty Mead

⅔ cup heavy (whipping) cream

½ teaspoon Worcestershire sauce

½ cup (2 ounces) grated Kerrygold Dubliner cheese

In a small bowl, blend the butter, mustard, garlic, chives, and salt and pepper to taste. Spread an equal portion on each slice of bread. Fit 8 slices, buttered side down, into the bottom of a 9-by-13-inch glass baking dish. Sprinkle the Blarney and Swiss cheese over the bread. Place the remaining bread, buttered side up, on top of the cheese.

In a medium bowl, whisk together the eggs, milk, mead, cream, and Worcestershire sauce until well blended. Pour over the bread. Cover tightly with plastic wrap and refrigerate for at least 12 hours and up to 24 hours.

Preheat the oven to 350°F. Remove the baking dish from the refrigerator, uncover, and bake for 45 minutes. Sprinkle with the grated Dubliner cheese and continue to bake for 10 to 15 minutes longer, or until lightly browned and set. Remove from the oven and let rest for 15 to 20 minutes. Cut into bite-size squares and serve warm.

Note: If using the Kerrygold Garlic and Herb Butter, omit the garlic and the chives.

TURNIP GRATIN

1 pound small white turnips, peeled	Freshly ground pepper
2 tablespoons salt	1 cup heavy (whipping) cream
3 tablespoons unsalted Kerrygold Irish butter	2 ounces (½ cup) shredded Kerrygold Vintage Cheddar cheese
1 shallot, minced	2 tablespoons fresh white bread crumbs (see Note, page 25)
¼ cup dried parsley	

Grate the turnips on the large side of a box grater, or shred in a food processor. Transfer to a colander, sprinkle with the salt, and let stand for 10 to 15 minutes. Squeeze out the excess moisture.

In a medium skillet over medium heat, melt the butter. Sauté the shallot for 2 to 3 minutes, or until soft but not browned. Stir in the grated turnip, toss to coat, and cook for 8 to 10 minutes, or until tender. Sprinkle with the parsley and pepper to taste. Stir in the cream, reduce the heat to low, and simmer for 10 to 12 minutes, or until the cream is reduced and the mixture has thickened.

Preheat the broiler. Transfer to 4 individual broiler-safe gratin dishes, sprinkle with the cheese and bread crumbs, and broil, 4 inches from the heat source, for about 1 minute, or until the top is browned and the mixture is bubbling.

Medieval Castle Banquets

Bunratty, Knappogue, and Dunguaire castles were once noble homes of Irish lords, a rank that was the zenith of medieval achievement and power. These castles, much like the medieval and Renaissance courts throughout Europe, were the hub around which the lives of Irish peasants, artisans, poets, and musicians revolved.

Visitors today can experience a taste of what dining in such surroundings must have been like. Since 1963, when Bunratty was the first of the three castles to be restored, medieval banquets (known collectively as Shannon Heritage banquets) have been held nightly, offering original entertainment, legendary Irish hospitality, and fine food and drink in fairy-tale settings.

At Bunratty Castle, located on the main Ennis-Limerick Road in County Clare, visitors are the guests of the Earl of Thomond, once the master of the superbly restored fifteenth-century castle. During the four decades since the famous banquets began, Bunratty's accomplished musicians have gained worldwide recognition and have performed for countless visitors and many distinguished heads of state.

The twice-nightly banquets begin with a formal greeting by the earl and his court, a welcoming glass of honey-rich mead (produced in the Bunratty Winery at the rear of the castle), and a four-course meal accompanied by fine wines.

Entertainment is provided between courses. At Bunratty they describe the banquet as "food from the rich earth, music made in heaven." At Knappogue Castle, in Quin, County Clare, the entertainment takes the form of a tribute in song, story, and dance to the women of Ireland: its imperious queens, inspirational saints, and occasional sinners. The music and poetry celebrate the gentle aspects of Ireland's past and the influential role of the women of Celtic Ireland. The castle, a legacy of the McNamara clan, who built it in 1467, has held medieval banquets since 1967. The castle banquets are offered nightly from May to October.

The medieval banquet at Dunguaire Castle, in Kinvara, County Galway, offers "food to please the palate and entertainment to lift the soul." The castle itself, built by the Hynes clan in 1520, is an inspirational place, occupying a site on the shore of Galway Bay that was a seventh-century stronghold of the kings of Connaught. The players at Dunguaire celebrate some of Ireland's greatest writers—Synge, Yeats, Shaw, and O'Casey among them—and draw on Irish history, myth, and legend for their inspiration. While the banquet meal is served, artists entertain with the profound, humorous, irreverent, and incisive words of some of Ireland's literary giants (see Resources, page 151).

CRAGGAUNOWEN CHICKEN

This dish is named in honor of Craggaunowen, "the living past," a heritage site near Quin, in County Clare. The site, which is operated by Shannon Heritage, tells the story of the arrival of the Celts in Ireland and the many changes they wrought upon daily life. A major feature of the visit is a *crannog* (meaning "young tree"), which is a reconstructed lake dwelling of a type found in Ireland during the Iron Age and early Christian periods. The site also includes a ring fort, a true reproduction of a farmer's house, an Iron Age roadway, and an outdoor cooking site. This recipe is modeled after the chicken with apple and mead sauce served at the legendary medieval banquets in the area, also operated by Shannon Heritage (see page 109 and Resources, page 151). It's delicious served with Irish Apple-Potato Cakes.

SERVES 6 AS A MAIN COURSE

---

6 boneless chicken breasts, 5 to 6 ounces each

½ cup finely chopped white mushrooms

½ cup fresh white bread crumbs (see Note, page 25)

½ teaspoon dried tarragon

1 tablespoon minced fresh flat-leaf parsley

5 tablespoons golden raisins

5 tablespoons chopped walnuts

1 small Granny Smith apple, unpeeled, cored and finely chopped

Salt and freshly ground pepper

1 cup Bunratty Mead

6 tablespoons unsalted Kerrygold Irish butter, melted

1 cup homemade chicken stock or canned low-sodium chicken broth

Irish Apple-Potato Cakes (page 88) for serving (optional)

Fresh parsley sprigs for garnish

Preheat the oven to 350°F. Lightly grease a 2-quart casserole dish.

Place the chicken breasts between 2 sheets of wax paper and, with a mallet or rolling pin, pound or roll them to a ½-inch thickness. In a medium bowl, combine the mushrooms, bread crumbs, tarragon, parsley, raisins, walnuts, apple, and salt and pepper to taste. Stir in ½ cup of the mead and 3 tablespoons of the melted butter. If necessary, add a little more butter to moisten.

Lay the chicken breasts on a work surface and brush the tops with some of the remaining melted butter. Season with salt and pepper to taste. Place 1 tablespoon of stuffing in the center of each breast. Fold in the sides, envelope style, and roll up. Place seam side down in the prepared dish. Brush again with the remaining melted butter and bake for 15 minutes. Mix the remaining ½ cup mead with the stock or broth and pour over the chicken. Cook, basting 2 or 3 times, for 25 to 30 minutes, or until the chicken is no longer pink inside. Remove from the oven and serve immediately with the sauce spooned over the top. Serve with apple-potato cakes, if desired, and garnish with parsley sprigs.

TULACH MHÓR LAMB CASSEROLE

Tullamore, a busy town in County Offaly, in the Midlands area of Ireland, is the modern name for Tullach Mhór, meaning "hill" or "mound." Today the county capital is the location of the Tullamore Dew Heritage Centre, where the famous whiskey was first produced in 1829 (see page 25 and Resources, page 151) and where Irish Mist was developed in the 1940s. This recipe is from "The Legendary Liqueur," a food and drinks booklet produced by the makers of Irish Mist nearly three decades ago. If you wish, serve this casserole with Rutabaga Purée or Turnip Gratin.

SERVES 6 TO 8 AS A MAIN COURSE

---

1 ¾ cups homemade chicken stock or canned low-sodium chicken broth

½ cup Irish Mist liqueur

4 large baking potatoes, peeled and sliced

2 pounds lamb, cut into 1 ½-inch pieces

3 medium onions, sliced

Salt and freshly ground pepper

1 teaspoon fresh thyme leaves

Minced fresh flat-leaf parsley for garnish

Rutabaga Purée (facing page) or Turnip Gratin (page 108) for serving (optional)

Preheat the oven to 350°F. Generously butter a 3-quart casserole dish.

In a medium bowl, whisk together the stock or broth and liqueur. Set aside. Place one of the sliced potatoes in the bottom of the prepared dish. Cover with one-third of the lamb and one of the sliced onions. Sprinkle with salt and pepper to taste, and the thyme. Repeat the layering until all has been used, ending with the potatoes. Pour the stock mixture over all, cover with aluminum foil, and bake for about 1 ½ hours, or until the potatoes and lamb are tender. Uncover and cook for 20 minutes longer, or until the top is browned.

To serve, spoon into shallow bowls and sprinkle with the parsley. Serve with the rutabaga purée or turnip gratin, if desired.

RUTABAGA PURÉE

Much confusion surrounds the origin, even the identity, of turnips, which are also called rutabagas or Swedes. Most varieties of turnip are white-fleshed and most varieties of rutabaga are yellow-fleshed, but there are also white-fleshed rutabagas and yellow-fleshed turnips, to further add to the confusion. Regardless of the name, a purée of this rough-skinned vegetable makes an excellent accompaniment to many meat dishes, and it's an extremely popular vegetable in Ireland.

SERVES 4 TO 6 AS A SIDE DISH

3 pounds rutabagas, peeled and cut into 1-inch pieces

4 tablespoons unsalted Kerrygold Irish butter

Sea salt and freshly ground pepper

Cook the rutabagas in a large pot of boiling salted water for 45 to 50 minutes, or until tender. Drain. Return to the pot to dry out a bit. Transfer to a blender or food processor, and process until smooth. (Or use an immersion blender and blend until smooth.) Stir in the butter and season to taste with salt and pepper.

PARKNASILLA PORK CHOPS

Beautifully situated in the midst of sea, woods, and mountains, Parknasilla is located on the scenic Ring of Kerry overlooking the Kenmare River. Because of the effects of the Gulf Stream and the sheltered location, the area has a delightful climate where subtropical plants and vegetation flourish. While you will not find pineapples—one of the key ingredients in this recipe—growing here, you will be delighted by the flavor of this pork chop dish sweetened with honey and mead. Serve with Crushed Potatoes.

SERVES 6 AS A MAIN COURSE

¼ cup all-purpose flour	6 pineapple slices
Salt and freshly ground pepper	½ cup pineapple juice
6 center-cut pork chops, ¾ inch thick	¼ cup honey
2 tablespoons canola oil	¼ cup Bunratty Mead
1 tablespoon Dijon mustard	Crushed Potatoes (page 21) for serving
1 tablespoon light brown sugar	

Preheat the oven to 350°F. Grease a baking dish large enough to hold the pork chops.

In a shallow bowl, combine the flour and salt and pepper to taste. Coat the chops with the mixture and shake off the excess.

In a large skillet over medium heat, heat the oil. Cook the chops for 3 minutes on each side, or until browned. Transfer to the prepared dish.

In a small bowl, whisk together the mustard and brown sugar. Spread the mustard mixture over each chop and top with a pineapple slice. In another small bowl, whisk together the pineapple juice, honey, and mead and spoon it over the chops. Cover the dish with aluminum foil and bake for 30 minutes. Uncover and bake for 30 minutes longer, or until an instant-read thermometer inserted into the center of a chop registers 145°F.

To serve, place a chop in the center of each of 6 plates and spoon the sauce over the top. Serve with the potatoes.

CRATLOE HILLS CHEESE SALAD with MUSTARD-MEAD VINAIGRETTE

Those familiar with the area around Bunratty will recognize this salad as a tribute to County Clare. The mead used in the vinaigrette is made directly behind the castle, and Cratloe Hills, a sheep's cheese, is made just down the road. It was named "best Irish cheese" at the 2004 British Cheese awards, with tasting notes there describing it as "a bold, terracotta-colored truckle with a rustic elegance; each bite revealing a complexity of flavors, such as apple, roasted onion, and burnt caramel." No wonder it's such a great addition to this salad. If sheep's cheese is not available where you live, you can substitute goat cheese.

SERVES 4 AS A STARTER

Mustard-Mead Vinaigrette	Salad
⅓ cup extra-virgin olive oil	Four 1-inch-thick slices Cratloe Hills sheep's cheese, or goat cheese
1 tablespoon cider vinegar	¼ cup olive oil
3 tablespoons Bunratty Mead	¾ cup fresh white bread crumbs (see Note, page 25)
2 tablespoons Dijon mustard	10 ounces mixed salad greens
1 tablespoon minced shallot	¼ cup dried cranberries
½ teaspoon freshly ground pepper	¼ cup chopped walnuts

To make the vinaigrette: Combine all the ingredients in a sealable jar and shake to blend. Set aside.

To make the salad: Place the cheese in a small bowl and spoon the oil over the top. Turn the cheese to coat both sides. Refrigerate for 4 hours.

Preheat the oven to 400°F. Lightly oil a baking sheet.

Place the bread crumbs in a small bowl. Remove the cheese from the refrigerator and dredge in the crumbs. Transfer the cheese to the baking sheet and bake, without turning, for 8 to 10 minutes, or until the cheese is lightly browned. In a medium bowl, toss the salad greens with the vinaigrette. Divide the greens among 4 plates. Remove the cheese from the oven and place 1 piece on top of each salad. Sprinkle with the dried cranberries and nuts.

SUMMER FRUIT COMPOTE with CELTIC SABAYON

DESSERTS

One of Italy's great gifts to the dessert world is zabaglione, a heavenly combination of egg yolks, sugar, and Marsala wine whisked over simmering water to a pale yellow froth. In France and other parts of the world, the sauce is called sabayon. Thanks to the world of Irish spirits, there's a new version made with Celtic Crossing, a blend of spirits, honey, and Cognac.

SERVES 6

Celtic Sabayon	Compote
4 egg yolks	1 cup raspberries
¼ cup superfine sugar	1 cup strawberries, hulled and sliced
3 tablespoons Celtic Crossing liqueur	1 cup blackberries
¾ cup dry white wine	1 cup blueberries
2 teaspoons fresh lemon juice	
	Confectioners' sugar for dusting
	Mint sprigs for garnish

To make the sabayon: In a double boiler, combine all the ingredients. Place over simmering, not boiling, water and whisk for 8 to 10 minutes, or until thick, pale, and creamy.

To make the compote: Preheat the broiler. Divide the fruit among six 8-ounce broiler-safe bowls. Spoon the sabayon over the top and brown lightly under the broiler 4 inches from the heat source for about 2 minutes, or use a kitchen blowtorch and move the flame constantly over the surface until the top is lightly browned. Dust with confectioners' sugar and garnish with sprigs of mint.

PINEAPPLE UPSIDE-DOWN CAKES

A favorite old-fashioned dessert is pineapple upside-down cake, where the sweet, caramelized bottom eventually becomes the colorful top. A slice from a can of sliced pineapples is a perfect fit for an individual ramekin, so this recipe offers great party potential. The smooth toffee and honey overtones of Eblana, from the makers of Cooley whiskey, add great flavor to the topping.

SERVES 8

Topping	Cake
4 tablespoons unsalted Kerrygold Irish butter	½ cup sweetened flaked coconut
⅓ cup light brown sugar	1½ cups all-purpose flour
2 tablespoons Eblana liqueur	½ teaspoon baking powder
8 pineapple slices, drained, from a 20-ounce can of pineapple slices	¼ teaspoon baking soda
8 maraschino cherries	½ teaspoon salt
	½ cup (1 stick) unsalted Kerrygold Irish butter, at room temperature
	1 cup granulated sugar
	1 large egg
	1 teaspoon vanilla extract
	¾ cup buttermilk

Preheat the oven 350°F. Generously butter eight 8-ounce ramekins.

To make the topping: In a small saucepan over medium-low heat, combine the butter, brown sugar, and liqueur. Cook, stirring constantly, for 5 to 6 minutes, or until the sugar has melted and the mixture is smooth. Divide the mixture among the prepared ramekins. Place a pineapple slice over the syrup in each one, and put a cherry in the center. Set aside.

To make the cake: In a small skillet over medium heat, toast the coconut, stirring frequently, for 2 to 3 minutes, or until it begins to lightly brown. Remove from the heat and let cool. In a large bowl, stir together the flour, baking powder, baking soda, and salt. Set aside.

CONTINUED

PINEAPPLE UPSIDE-DOWN CAKES continued

In a large bowl, beat the butter and granulated sugar with an electric mixer until light and fluffy. Beat in the egg and vanilla. Beat in half the flour mixture and half the buttermilk until well combined, then beat in the remaining flour and buttermilk until smooth. Stir in the coconut. Spoon the batter into the prepared ramekins and place them on a baking sheet.

Bake for 28 to 30 minutes, or until the tops are golden brown. Remove from the oven and let cool on a wire rack for 5 minutes. Run a knife around the sides of the ramekins and invert onto 8 dessert plates. Serve warm or at room temperature.

ROASTED RHUBARB TRIFLE

Toppings made with whiskey-based liqueurs can turn simple dishes into dazzling desserts. The honey-enhanced spirits are especially delicious when combined with fresh fruit in soufflés, in compotes, and in this trifle, which uses cooked rhubarb instead of traditional fruits and berries.

SERVES 6

---

3 to 4 stalks rhubarb, cut into 1½-inch slices

Grated zest of 1 orange

⅓ cup sugar

3 to 4 slices Cream Cheese Pound Cake (page 99), cut into 1-inch pieces

6 tablespoons Irish Mist liqueur

2 cups Crème Anglaise (see Note)

2 tablespoons finely chopped hazelnuts

Preheat the oven to 325°F. Put the rhubarb in a 3-quart casserole dish and sprinkle it with the orange zest and sugar. Cover with aluminum foil and bake for 30 to 40 minutes, or until tender. Remove from the oven and let the rhubarb cool completely.

Divide the pieces of pound cake among 6 wineglasses or goblets. Spoon 1 tablespoon of the liqueur over each. Spoon some of the rhubarb into each glass and cover with the crème anglaise. Refrigerate for at least 1 hour. Just before serving, sprinkle the hazelnuts over the custard.

Note: The recipe for crème anglaise (page 42) contains whiskey. For this recipe, omit it, or make crème anglaise using custard powder such as Bird's (see Resources, page 151).

Mead: The Wedding Story

While the origin of the words "wedding," "bride," and "groom" have been traced back as far as the ninth century, young men have been "wooing" young women only since the eleventh century, about the same time they first called each other "dear." Marriage in the Middle Ages was quite different than it is today, and when people spoke of a good match, they were referring more to what someone could bring to the union in the way of possessions, rather than possibilities.

The word "honeymoon," however, may be older than most wedding-related terms, and didn't evolve from a term of endearment or a description of an event. Instead, it referred to the month, or full moon, after a wedding.

In the Middle Ages, Irish monks produced the honey-based mead for medicinal purposes, but it was believed that mead was essential for giving the bride and groom a good send-off after the wedding. It was used both as a final toast and as a proper beginning of the marriage. Following the wedding, the bride and groom were provided with enough mead to toast each other after their wedding for one full moon, hence the term "honeymoon." This delicate yet potent drink was not only considered the best way to start a new marriage, it was also believed to enhance fertility and virility.

According to Irish tradition, when it's time to bring the festivities to a close, the wedding party gathers around the bride and groom, fills their glasses with mead, and recites this toast: "Friends and relatives, so fond and dear, 'tis our greatest pleasure to have seen you here. When many years this day has passed, fondest memories will always last. So we drink a cup of Irish mead, and ask God's blessing in your hour of need."

The family and guests raise their glasses of mead and respond, "On this your special day, our wish to you; the goodness of the old, the best of the new. God bless you both who drink this mead; may it always fill your every need."

RASPBERRY-MEAD SWISS ROLL

This recipe was originally made with gooseberries, a very Irish but not very accessible fruit. I find that raspberries, and even strawberries, are a perfect and more colorful substitute. They also remind me of the jelly rolls my mother used to make, which she spread with raspberry jam. The mead adds a honey-like sweetness.

SERVES 8 TO 10

Cake	Filling
¾ cup all-purpose flour	1 cup raspberries
1 teaspoon baking powder	¼ cup granulated sugar
¼ teaspoon salt	1 tablespoon water
3 large eggs	3 tablespoons Bunratty Mead
1 cup granulated sugar	⅔ cup heavy (whipping) cream
⅓ cup water	
½ teaspoon vanilla extract	Fresh raspberries for garnish
Confectioners' sugar for dusting	

To make the cake: Preheat the oven to 375°F. Line a 15-by-10-by-1-inch jelly roll pan with wax paper. Spray the paper with cooking oil spray.

In a small bowl, sift together the flour, baking powder, and salt. In a large bowl, beat the eggs and granulated sugar with an electric mixer for about 5 minutes, or until thick and lemon colored. Beat in the water and vanilla, and then add the flour mixture. Pour the batter into the prepared pan. Smooth the top with a spatula and spread the batter to the corners.

Bake the cake for 12 to 15 minutes, or until golden and the center springs back when lightly touched. Remove from the oven and invert the pan onto a clean kitchen towel that has been dusted with confectioners' sugar. Gently peel off the wax paper and dust the cake with confectioners' sugar. Starting from a short side, gently roll up the cake with the towel. Place, seam side down, on a wire rack, and let cool for 30 minutes or longer while you prepare the filling.

To make the filling: In a small saucepan over medium heat, combine the raspberries, granulated sugar, and water. Cook for 5 to 7 minutes, or until the raspberries begin to break up. Remove from the heat and let cool. Transfer to a small bowl, stir in 1 tablespoon of the mead, and refrigerate for 20 minutes.

In a large bowl, whip the cream with an electric mixer until soft peaks form. Fold in the raspberry mixture. Unroll the cake and remove the towel. Spread the cake with the filling, leaving about a ¼-inch border, and carefully reroll the cake. Cover with plastic wrap and refrigerate for at least 2 hours.

To serve, drizzle the remaining 2 tablespoons mead over the top of the cake, dust with confectioners' sugar, and slice.

Garnish with raspberries.

PEARS POACHED in MEAD

Pears are often poached in red wine or port, which adds both color and flavor, but I find them even sweeter when the poaching liquid is made with Bunratty Mead. The silky cheese accompaniment—a blend of Irish blue cheese and Italian mascarpone, a soft, triple-cream cheese—is a luxurious addition.

SERVES 6

1 ¼ cups Bunratty Mead	Zest of 1 orange, cut into strips
¾ cup sugar	6 firm Bosc or Bartlett pears, peeled, stems intact
½ cup water	4 ounces mascarpone cheese
2 to 3 cinnamon sticks	4 ounces Cashel Blue cheese, crumbled

In a large saucepan over medium heat, bring the mead, sugar, water, cinnamon sticks, and orange zest to a boil. Cook for 6 to 8 minutes, or until the sugar dissolves and the mixture is syrupy. Reduce the heat to low, add the pears, and simmer, covered, for 25 to 35 minutes, or until the pears are tender. Turn the pears with tongs 2 or 3 times during cooking. Remove from the heat and let the pears cool in the poaching liquid. Strain the liquid into a bowl and set aside.

In a small bowl, whisk together the mascarpone and blue cheese until blended.

To serve, stand a pear in the center of each of 6 dessert plates, spoon some syrup over them, and place a dollop of the cheese mixture next to each.

IRISH MIST SOUFFLÉS with ORANGE SAUCE

Nearly every chef in Ireland has a favorite recipe for a dessert soufflé made with Irish Mist, the first of the whiskey liqueurs. The distinctive undertones of honey and herbs pair well with a citrus sauce like this one made with orange juice, orange zest, and lemon juice. It is customary to pull open the soufflés with a fork and spoon some of the sauce into the center.

SERVES 8

Orange Sauce	Soufflés
4 tablespoons unsalted Kerrygold Irish butter	6 tablespoons unsalted Kerrygold Irish butter
½ cup light brown sugar	5 tablespoons all-purpose flour
Grated zest of 2 oranges	1 cup milk
1 ½ cups fresh orange juice, strained to remove the pulp	7 large eggs, separated
⅛ teaspoon ground cloves	¼ teaspoon vanilla extract
1 tablespoon fresh lemon juice	Pinch of salt
1 tablespoon cornstarch	2 tablespoons Irish Mist liqueur
1 teaspoon vanilla extract	1 cup granulated sugar

To make the sauce: In a small saucepan over medium heat, melt the butter and brown sugar. Add the orange zest, then whisk in the orange juice and cloves. Reduce the heat to low and simmer for 1 to 2 minutes, or until blended. In a small bowl, whisk together the lemon juice and cornstarch, then whisk it into the orange mixture. Simmer for 3 to 5 minutes, or until the sauce thickens. Remove from the heat, strain through a fine-mesh sieve into a bowl, stir in the vanilla, and return to the saucepan to keep warm while preparing the soufflés.

To make the soufflés: Preheat the oven to 400°F. Butter eight 8-ounce ramekins and dust with granulated sugar, knocking out the excess.

In a large saucepan over medium-low heat, melt the butter. Whisk in the flour and cook for 2 to 3 minutes, or until smooth. Add the milk and cook, whisking constantly, for 3 to 4 minutes, or until the mixture is thick and smooth. Transfer the mixture to a medium bowl and let it cool for 5 minutes.

In a large bowl, whisk together the egg yolks, vanilla, and salt. Whisk in the milk mixture and the liqueur until smooth. In a second large bowl, beat the egg whites with an electric mixer until soft peaks form. Gradually beat in the granulated sugar until stiff peaks form. Whisk one-quarter of the egg whites into the yolk mixture to lighten, then fold in the remaining egg whites until well blended.

Spoon the batter into the prepared ramekins and place them in a large baking pan. Add enough hot water to come halfway up the sides of the dishes. Bake for 20 minutes, or until the tops are puffed and golden. Remove the pan from the oven, and with oven mitts, transfer each soufflé to a dessert plate.

To serve, split open the top of each soufflé with a fork and spoon in some sauce.

CHAPTER FIVE

Sweet Irish Creams

While the taste of Irish-made mead, whiskey, beer, and cider has been pleasing palates for centuries, the cream liqueurs of Ireland have been on the market for only three decades. Experts say their inception was as inevitable as tomorrow's rain, for it was only a matter of time before two of Ireland's greatest treasures—the cream from its rich dairy pastures and the spirits from its finest distilleries—would be brought together to create a third. It's the marriage of these two traditions that accounts for the unparalleled success of Irish cream liqueurs in the world market.

R & A Bailey launched its Original Irish Cream in 1974 after discovering the secret that would allow milk to be separated into double cream and blended with natural flavors, Irish whiskey, and neutral spirits. Steeped in Irish history and lore, it was named after the Bailey, a Dublin pub that was a favorite haunt of James Joyce. Its bottle design is based on an old Irish whiskey brand, Red Breast. The origins of Baileys,

in fact, assume near mythic proportions, with some claiming that the liqueur harkens back to a tradition in the west of Ireland where one "dropped a dab of fresh cream into some Irish whiskey, stirred, shook, and tossed it down." The idea of a bottled cream liqueur with "magical smoothness, subtle depth, and rich, heart-warming luxury" is the character that makes Baileys one of the world's premier liqueurs.

Following Baileys into the marketplace were Carolans Irish cream, named for the celebrated seventeenth-century blind harpist Turlough O'Carolan, and Emmets, named for the Irish patriot Robert Emmet. While the key ingredients in these are also whiskey and cream, Carolans adds a touch of honey to give it a distinctively subtle flavor that differentiates it from others. Honey is an appropriate ingredient in a drink produced in Clonmel, County Tipperary, as the name Clonmel is derived from the Gaelic *Cluain Meala*, meaning "vale of honey." In 1983, Saint

Baileys Historical Pub Crawl in Belfast

The Northern Ireland city of Belfast is well known for its many famous and historic pubs. To be sure you don't miss one, Baileys sponsors a two-hour tour led by a professional guide, who provides both history and humor along the way. But don't be put off by the thought of being led around as if you were on a school field trip. There's plenty of time to experience the *craic* (Irish for "good times") in each of the pubs and to enjoy some banter with the locals over a glass of the world's first Irish cream liqueur. Eleven historic pubs make up the itinerary, with six visited on a rotating basis.

The tour always begins at the Crown Saloon, on Great Victoria Street, which boasts one of the most perfectly preserved Victorian pub interiors in all of Ireland. Next stop might be the Blackthorn on Skipper Street, a genuine workingman's pub whose clientele ranges from dockworkers and journalists to accountants and warehouse men. Bittles Bar, at Victoria Square, is a curious triangular building decorated with gilded shamrocks and memorabilia celebrating Irish literary figures such as James Joyce, W. B. Yeats, and Oscar Wilde. On Commercial Street, once the heart of the city's newspaper district, the Duke of York is filled with the paraphernalia of the printing trade, with great screw presses and wall murals made entirely of hot metal type. The Garrick, on Chichester Street, is at the heart of the city's commercial district. The pub has been recently restored to reflect its former ambiance in the days when nearby streets were the city's Bohemian quarter. For details on the pub crawl, see Resources, page 151.

BAILEYS BOMBSHELL

Chef Dermot Moore is in charge of the kitchen at The Meetings, his family's pub in the picturesque Vale of Avoca, in County Wicklow. His straightforward cooking style is well balanced by his appreciation for local ingredients and proven methods of preparation. Although simplicity is the key to this recipe, the flavors are anything but simple! Feel free to add a few additional meringues for a more explosive texture in this "bombshell" dessert, which he sweetens with a healthy dose of Baileys Irish cream liqueur. For a fruity "bombshell," you might like to try the variation, which uses Carolans Irish cream (variation follows).

SERVES 8

---

2 cups heavy (whipping) cream

½ cup Baileys Irish cream liqueur

One 5-ounce package meringues (see Note)

4 ounces semisweet (not bittersweet) chocolate, grated

Fresh strawberries, hulled and halved, for garnish

Line a 9-by-5-by 3-inch metal loaf pan with parchment or wax paper long enough to wrap back over the top. In a large bowl, beat the cream and liqueur with an electric mixer until stiff peaks form. Crumble the meringues into small pieces and fold them into the whipped cream. Stir in the grated chocolate. Spoon the mixture into the prepared pan and freeze overnight.

To serve, uncover the pan and invert onto a serving plate. Remove the paper. Cut the dessert into slices and garnish with strawberries.

Variation

Carolans Strawberry and Meringue Crunch: In a large bowl, beat 1¼ cups heavy (whipping) cream, 1 tablespoon sugar, and ¼ cup Carolans Irish cream with an electric mixer until stiff peaks form. Crumble a 5-ounce package of meringues into small pieces and fold into the whipped cream. In a medium bowl, combine 3 tablespoons sugar and 6 ounces hulled fresh strawberries (reserve a few for garnish), and crush the berries with a fork. Fold the strawberries into the cream mixture. Spoon into 4 stemmed glasses or goblets and refrigerate for 2 to 3 hours. Garnish with the reserved strawberries and a few sprigs of fresh mint.

SERVES 4

Note: Miss Meringue brand, which is widely available in U.S. supermarkets, is a great substitute for homemade meringues. They were created by a French chef, who took a traditional meringue recipe and created a cookie that is free of fat, artificial colors, and preservatives (see Resources, page 151).

BROWN BREAD ICE CREAM

Many cooks have found that the sweet cream liqueurs of Ireland combine beautifully with another staple, brown soda bread, to create a sumptuous ice cream. In fact, brown bread ice cream is so popular that cooks often bake a second loaf, freeze it, and reserve it to use for bread crumbs in this ice cream, or as a crunchy topping for fruit cobblers.

SERVES 4 TO 6

2 cups Brown Soda Bread crumbs (page 81)	½ cup confectioners' sugar
¼ cup light brown sugar	½ teaspoon vanilla extract
1 ¼ cups heavy (whipping) cream	3 tablespoons Irish cream liqueur
⅔ cup half-and-half	

Preheat the oven to 375°F. Line a baking sheet with aluminum foil.

In a small bowl, toss the bread crumbs with the brown sugar. Spread the crumb mixture out on the prepared baking sheet and bake, stirring occasionally to prevent sticking, for 10 to 15 minutes, or until the crumbs are golden and caramelized. Remove from the oven and let cool. Scrape the crumbs into a resealable plastic bag and, with a rolling pin, crush the crumbs into small pieces.

In a large bowl, whip the cream and half-and-half with an electric mixer until stiff peaks form. Fold in the confectioners' sugar, vanilla, liqueur, and bread crumbs. Process in a 1-quart ice cream maker according to the manufacturer's directions. Transfer to a plastic container and freeze until ready to serve.

BAILEYS CHOCOLATE POTS

This rich, smooth chocolate dessert reminds you of a French *pot de crème au chocolate*. Devised by Georgina O'Sullivan of Bord Bia (the Irish Food Board), it gets its own national identity from the addition of Baileys Irish cream liqueur. Serve these little pots with some fresh strawberries, Mrs. McCann's Oatmeal Cookies, or delicate Irish Lace Cookies.

SERVES 6

---

1 cup heavy (whipping) cream

5 ounces unsweetened chocolate, broken into small pieces

1 large egg, beaten

1 tablespoon Baileys Irish cream liqueur

Mrs. McCann's Oatmeal Cookies (page 140) for serving

Irish Lace Cookies (page 141) for serving

In a small saucepan over medium heat, heat the cream to almost boiling. Reduce the heat to low, add the chocolate, and simmer for 5 to 7 minutes, or until the chocolate is melted and the mixture is smooth. Whisk in the egg and liqueur and cook for 2 to 3 minutes, or until the mixture thickens. Pour the mixture into six 4-ounce ramekins and refrigerate for at least 24 hours, or until the puddings are set. Serve with oatmeal or lace cookies.

MRS. McCANN'S OATMEAL COOKIES

MAKES ABOUT 4 DOZEN COOKIES

1¼ cups (2½ sticks) unsalted Kerrygold Irish butter, at room temperature

½ cup packed brown sugar

½ cup granulated sugar

1 large egg, beaten

1 teaspoon vanilla extract

1½ cups all-purpose flour

1 teaspoon baking soda

1 teaspoon salt

1 teaspoon cinnamon

3 cups McCann's quick-cooking (not instant) Irish oatmeal

¾ cup raisins

½ cup chopped walnuts (optional)

Preheat the oven to 350°F. Line 2 baking sheets with parchment paper.

In a large bowl, beat the butter and sugars with an electric mixer until light and fluffy. Beat in the egg and vanilla. Stir in the flour, baking soda, salt, and cinnamon. Mix well. With a wooden spoon, stir in the oatmeal, raisins, and walnuts, if using. Drop rounded teaspoons of batter onto the prepared cookie sheets, leaving space between them. Bake for 12 to 15 minutes, or until golden brown. Remove from the oven and let cool for 5 minutes. Transfer to a wire rack.

IRISH LACE COOKIES

MAKES ABOUT 2 DOZEN COOKIES

½ cup (1 stick) unsalted Kerrygold Irish butter, at room temperature

¾ cup light brown sugar

2 tablespoons all-purpose flour

2 tablespoons milk

1 teaspoon vanilla extract

1¼ cups McCann's quick-cooking (not instant) oatmeal

Preheat the oven to 350°F.

In a large bowl, beat the butter and brown sugar with an electric mixer until light and fluffy. Beat in the flour, milk, and vanilla. Stir in the oatmeal. Let the batter rest for 15 minutes.

Drop the batter by 6 rounded teaspoons onto 2 ungreased cookie sheets, spacing them 3 inches apart. Bake for 10 to 12 minutes, or until the cookies have spread and are golden. Remove the cookies from the oven and let rest for 1 to 2 minutes, or until they are firm enough to be moved with a metal spatula. Transfer to a wire rack to cool completely. Repeat with the remaining dough.

CHOCOLATE CAKE with BRADY'S and BERRIES

Brady's Irish cream liqueur is made in a small batch process and is bottled within 48 hours of the cream reaching the distillery. Unlike many Irish creams, Brady's is made with Irish single malt whiskey as well as neutral grain spirits. The natural flavors of dark chocolate and vanilla combine to give Brady's a distinctive, lush taste, which marries well with the chocolate in this cake.

LAYER CAKE SERVES 8 TO 10; MARY ANN CAKE SERVES 12 TO 14

Cake	Filling
2 ¼ cups plus 2 tablespoons cake flour	1 ¼ cups heavy (whipping) cream
1 tablespoon baking powder	3 tablespoons Brady's Irish cream liqueur
¾ teaspoon salt	3 cups mixed berries, such as sliced strawberries, raspberries, and blueberries
1 ½ cups superfine sugar	
⅔ cup plus 2 tablespoons unsweetened cocoa powder	
1 cup boiling water	Confectioners' sugar for dusting
3 large eggs	Mint leaves for garnish
2 teaspoons vanilla extract	
¾ cup (1 ½ sticks) unsalted Kerrygold Irish butter, at room temperature	
¼ cup Brady's Irish cream liqueur	

To make the cake: Preheat the oven to 350°F. Grease two 9-inch round cake pans or a Mary Ann cake pan (see Note) and dust with cocoa powder.

In a large bowl, sift together the flour, baking powder, and salt. Stir in the superfine sugar. Set aside. In a small bowl, whisk together the cocoa and water until smooth. Set aside.

In a large bowl, beat the eggs, ¼ cup of the cocoa mixture, and vanilla with an electric mixer until light and fluffy. In a separate bowl, combine the dry ingredients, butter, and remaining cocoa mixture. Beat on low speed for 1 to 2 minutes, or until blended. Add the egg mixture in thirds, beating well after each addition. Stir in the liqueur.

Spoon the batter into the prepared pan(s) and bake the round pans for 25 to 30 minutes, the Mary Ann pan for 43 to 45 minutes, or until the cake is risen and a skewer inserted in the center comes out clean.

Remove the cake(s) from the oven and transfer to a wire rack to cool for 10 minutes. Invert the cake(s) and remove the pan(s). Let cool completely.

To make the filling: In a medium bowl, whip the cream and liqueur with an electric mixer until soft peaks form. If you baked the cake in layers, spread half the whipped cream over one cake and top with half the berries. Place the other cake on top, spread with the remaining whipped cream, and arrange the remaining berries over the cream. If you baked the cake in the Mary Ann pan, spread all of the cream into the well of the cake and top with all the fruit. Dust with confectioners' sugar and garnish with mint leaves. Refrigerate for 30 minutes before cutting into slices.

Note: I made this as a traditional layer cake until I discovered the Mary Ann pan, a fluted cake pan first introduced in the United States in 1921. The pan, a version of which is available from Williams-Sonoma, a home furnishings company, has an inverted well, which is perfect for filling with berries and whipped cream (see Resources, page 151).

BAILEYS WHITE CHOCOLATE TART
with RASPBERRY COULIS

Martin Dwyer, chef-proprietor of Dwyer's, on Mary Street in Waterford, spent many years cooking in kitchens in France and England before returning to the sunny southeast of Ireland in 1989 to open his own restaurant. When R & A Bailey decided to invite chefs from around Ireland to contribute a recipe to its *Pure Indulgence* cookbook, Dwyer offered this decadent white chocolate tart, which he serves with a raspberry coulis.

SERVES 6

Pastry	Raspberry Coulis
2 cups all-purpose flour	4 ounces raspberries, plus a few for garnish
2 tablespoons superfine sugar	1 tablespoon water
½ cup (1 stick) unsalted Kerrygold Irish butter	
1 large egg yolk, beaten with 2 tablespoons water	Fresh mint sprigs for garnish
Filling	
8 ounces (8 squares) white chocolate	
½ cup (1 stick) unsalted Kerrygold Irish butter	
3 tablespoons Baileys Irish cream liqueur	
2 large eggs	
3 large egg yolks	
1 tablespoon honey	

To make the pastry: Combine the flour, sugar, and butter in a food processor, and pulse 5 to 6 times, or until the mixture resembles coarse crumbs. Add half of the egg yolk mixture, and process until a soft dough forms. Form the dough into a ball, wrap in plastic wrap, and refrigerate for 1 hour.

Preheat the oven to 400°F. Roll out the dough between 2 sheets of wax paper to a thickness of ¼ inch. Line a 12-inch tart pan with the dough, leaving a small overlap in case of shrinkage. Cover the dough with a piece of aluminum foil, fill it with pie weights, and bake for 15 minutes. Remove the weights and foil, brush with the remaining egg wash, and bake for 3 to 5 minutes longer, or until lightly browned. Remove from the oven and set aside. Reduce the oven temperature to 350°F.

CONTINUED

BAILEYS WHITE CHOCOLATE TART with RASPBERRY COULIS continued

To make the filling: In a small saucepan over medium heat, melt the chocolate and butter. Stir in the liqueur, remove from the heat, and let cool for 20 minutes. In a large bowl, beat the whole eggs, egg yolks, and honey with an electric mixer until light and fluffy. Whisk the chocolate mixture into the egg mixture and pour into the pastry shell. Bake for 30 minutes, or until the filling is set and the top is golden. Remove from the oven and let cool completely on a wire rack.

To make the coulis: In a small saucepan over medium heat, combine the raspberries and water. Cook for 5 to 8 minutes, or until the berries break down. Transfer the mixture to a food processor and purée until smooth. Strain the mixture through a fine-mesh sieve into a bowl and let cool.

To serve, drizzle some of the coulis onto 6 serving plates, cut the tart into slices, and put a slice on each plate. Garnish each with a few whole raspberries and a sprig of mint.

SAINT BRENDAN'S OATMEAL–CHOCOLATE MINT COOKIES

Old-fashioned chocolate chip cookies never tasted this good! The Irish cream liqueur gives these an additional richness, and the minty chocolate chips provide a unique flavor. Adults might even like to dunk them in a glass of Irish cream liqueur for further indulgence.

MAKES ABOUT 4 DOZEN COOKIES

1¼ cups McCann's quick-cooking (not instant) oatmeal

1½ cups all-purpose flour

1 teaspoon baking powder

1 teaspoon baking soda

¾ teaspoon salt

1 cup (2 sticks) unsalted Kerrygold Irish butter, at room temperature

1 cup light brown sugar

½ cup granulated sugar

1 large egg

¼ cup Saint Brendan's Irish cream liqueur

1 teaspoon vanilla extract

12 ounces mint chocolate chips, such as Hershey's brand, or mint chocolate, broken into small pieces

Preheat the oven to 350°F. Line 2 baking sheets with parchment paper.

Combine the oatmeal, flour, baking powder, baking soda, and salt in a food processor. Process for 10 to 15 seconds, or until the oats are finely ground.

In a large bowl, beat the butter and sugars with an electric mixer until light and fluffy. Beat in the egg, liqueur, and vanilla. On low speed, gradually beat in the flour mixture. Stir in the chocolate chips. If very soft, chill for approximately 15 to 20 minutes.

Drop by heaping teaspoons 2 inches apart onto the prepared pans. Bake for 10 to 12 minutes, or until the edges of the cookies are lightly browned. Remove from the oven and let cool for 2 minutes. With a spatula, transfer the cookies to a wire rack to cool completely. Repeat with the remaining dough.

CHOCOLATE CREAM SAUCE

MAKES ABOUT 2 1/2 CUPS

3 tablespoons cornstarch	2 cups heavy (whipping) cream
2 cups water	2 tablespoons Irish cream liqueur
2 tablespoons sugar	
1 ounce (1 square) semisweet chocolate, broken into small pieces	

In a small saucepan over medium heat, bring the cornstarch and water to a boil, whisking constantly. Reduce the heat to low and simmer for 2 to 3 minutes, or until smooth. Stir in the sugar and chocolate and cook for 2 to 3 minutes, or until the chocolate is melted and the sauce is smooth. Whisk in the cream and liqueur. Cook for 2 to 3 minutes, or until heated through. Serve hot.

COFFEE CREAM SAUCE

MAKES ABOUT 3 CUPS

1 cup light brown sugar	2 1/2 cups freshly brewed coffee
1/4 cup water	1/4 cup Irish cream liqueur

In a small saucepan over medium heat, bring the sugar and water to a boil, whisking constantly. Cook for 3 to 5 minutes, or until the mixture is syrupy. Whisk in the coffee and cook for 3 to 5 minutes, or until the sauce thickens. Remove from the heat and whisk in the liqueur. Serve hot.

PROFITEROLES

My mother made cream puffs as a special occasion dessert. I'm sure she didn't know that many cooks call them by their French name, profiteroles, and frankly, we didn't care. We loved them any way she served them, which was usually filled with freshly whipped cream or custard and topped with hot chocolate sauce. This updated recipe suggests two toppings—chocolate and coffee—both made with Irish cream liqueurs.

MAKES ABOUT 20 PROFITEROLES

1 cup water	4 large eggs
½ cup (1 stick) unsalted Kerrygold Irish butter	Créme Anglaise (page 42) or whipped cream for filling
1 teaspoon sugar	Chocolate Cream Sauce (facing page) or Coffee Cream Sauce (facing page) for serving
¼ teaspoon salt	
1 cup all-purpose flour	

Preheat the oven to 400°F. Line 2 baking sheets with parchment paper.

In a medium saucepan over medium-high heat, bring the water, butter, sugar, and salt to a boil. Add the flour all at once and stir vigorously with a wooden spoon until the mixture forms a ball and pulls away from the sides of the pan. Remove from the heat and add the eggs, one at a time, beating well after each addition.

Spoon the batter into a large pastry bag fitted with a ½-inch plain tip, and pipe about 10 puffs onto each prepared pan, spacing them about 1½ inches apart. Or drop the batter by rounded teaspoons onto the pans.

Bake for 30 to 35 minutes, rotating the baking sheets between upper and lower racks halfway through baking, or until puffed and golden. Remove from the oven and transfer to a wire rack to cool completely.

To serve, with a serrated knife, cut each profiterole in half horizontally. Remove and discard any moist dough inside. Spoon about 1 rounded tablespoon of créme anglaise or whipped cream into the bottom of each and replace the top. Arrange on dessert plates and drizzle with chocolate cream or coffee cream sauce.

GLOSSARY

Bacon
Traditional Irish bacon is available in a number of cuts, including the shoulder or collar (the traditional cut for bacon and cabbage), loin (most often used for back rashers or chops), streaky (also known as rashers and served as part of an Irish breakfast), or gammon (also known as ham).

Blue cheese
There are several producers of blue cheese in Ireland, including Cashel Blue, made in Fethard, County Tipperary, from the milk of pedigreed Friesian cows; Crozier Blue, also from the Grubb family, made from sheep's milk; Bellingham Blue, made in Castlebellingham, County Louth; and Kerrygold Blue, from the company that also produces Dubliner, Blarney, and Vintage Cheddar.

Coulis
A thick purée or sauce, often made with fruit.

Courgette
In Ireland, zucchini squash is called by its French name, *courgette*.

Irish cream liqueurs
Made from Irish whiskey, double cream, neutral spirits, and natural flavors, Irish cream liqueurs are frequently used in Irish cooking, especially desserts. Baileys Irish cream was the first one produced in Ireland.

Poitín
Distilled from barley, sugar, and water, poitín was originally made in pot stills over a peat fire. It was banned in Ireland in 1661 and was only recently legalized. Bunratty Poitín and Knockeen Hills Irish Poteen are now sold throughout the country as well as in the United States. Poitín is sometimes used as a substitute for Irish whiskey.

Porter
See Stout.

Stout
A strong, dark beer made with hops and dark-roasted barley. Guinness and Murphy's are Ireland's most popular stouts. Originally called porter, it was renamed stout by Arthur Guinness for its strong, bold taste.

Whole-wheat flour
In Ireland, whole-wheat flour, an important ingredient in Irish soda bread, is called whole-meal flour. To obtain the best texture, use extra-coarse whole-meal flour such as Odlum's or Howard's brand.

RESOURCES

Use this guide to find food and beverages from Ireland, ingredients called for in some recipes, or locations mentioned in this book.

To find an Irish shop in your area where some of these products are available, contact Enterprise Ireland, 345 Park Avenue, New York, NY 10154, phone 212-371-3600. Or try Bord Bia, the Irish Food Board, 400 North Michigan Avenue, Chicago, IL 60611, phone 773-871-6749, or visit them online at www.bordbia.ie.

For information on travel to Ireland, including accommodations, culture, sports, and festivals, contact Tourism Ireland, 345 Park Avenue, New York, NY 10154, phone 800-223-6470, or visit them online at www.tourismireland.com.

For information on a specific region of Ireland, visit online at www.corkkerry.ie for counties Cork and Kerry; www.visitdublin.com for Dublin city and county; www.ecoast-midlands.travel.ie for counties Kildare, Laois, Longford, Louth, Meath, North Offaly, Westmeath, and Wicklow; www.irelandnorthwest.ie for counties Cavan, Donegal, Leitrim, Monaghan, and Sligo; www.irelandwest.ie for counties Galway, Mayo, and Roscommon; www.shannonregiontourism.ie for counties Clare, Limerick, North Kerry, North Tipperary, and South Offaly, www.southeastireland.com for counties Carlow, Kildare, Tipperary, Waterford, and Wexford; www.discovernorthernireland.com for counties Antrim, Armagh, Derry, Down, Fermanagh, and Tyrone; and www.gotobelfast.com for Belfast.

Bacon
Depending on the cut of bacon required, traditional Irish bacon and ham can be found in many Irish butcher shops as well as from specialty grocers. To order, call Food Ireland, 877-IRISH-FOOD, or visit them online at www.foodireland.com; Irish Grub, www.irishgrub.com; Schaller & Weber, 212-879-3047, or visit them online at www.schallerweber.com.

Belfast Historical Pub Tour
Baileys Irish cream sponsors this tour of historic Belfast pubs. A professional guide, who provides both history and humor along the way, leads the tour. For details, visit the Belfast Tourist Office online at www.gotobelfast.com.

Biddy Early Brewery
This small pub-brewery is located a few miles outside of Inagh, in County Clare. For information on tours and tastings, visit them online at www.beb.ie.

Bird's Custard Powder
Bird's custard powder, available in most supermarkets, is the original custard brand, established in 1837. The powder is mixed with sugar and milk and can be used as a subsitute for crème anglaise.

Bulmers Irish Cider

Bulmers is Ireland's leading brand of cider. In the United States, the brand is Magners. For more information, visit them online at www.magners cider.com.

Bunratty Mead and Poitín

In Ireland, you can visit the Bunratty Winery, located directly behind Bunratty Castle, in County Clare, to see how mead and poitín are made. To find out where you can buy them in the United States, contact Camelot Importing Co., phone 800-4-CAMELOT.

Carlow Brewing Company

This microbrewery in Carlow, County Laois, makes several craft beers and stout. For more information, visit them online at www.carlow brewing.com.

Castle Brands

Castle Brands imports several products from Ireland, including Knappogue Castle single malt whiskey, Clontarf whiskey, Celtic Crossing liqueur, Brady's Irish cream, and Boru vodka. For more information, visit them online at www. castlebrandsinc.com.

Cider Industry Council

The Cider Industry Council was formed in 1988, and its members include the main manufacturers, distributors, and marketers of cider in Ireland. For information, visit them online at www.cider industrycouncil.com.

Farmhouse cheeses

To buy Irish farmhouse cheeses, contact Murrays Cheese Shop, 888-692-4339, or visit them online at www.murrayscheese.com; James Cook Cheese Company, 206-256-0510, or visit online at www.worldofcheese; or visit www.igourmet.com.

Guinness Storehouse

Ireland's number one paid visitor attraction, the Guinness Storehouse is a contemporary "museum" devoted to the history and production of Guinness stout, one of Ireland's most popular drinks. For information on tours and tastings, visit them online at www.guinness.com.

Hilden Brewery

Hilden, in the industrial town of Lisburn, in County Antrim, was Ireland's first independent brewing company. For information on tours and tastings, visit them online at www.hilden brewery.com.

Hot Irishman

To make Irish coffee, just add boiling water to Hot Irishman, a blend of coffee, sugar, and Irish whiskey. For more information, visit them online at www.hotirishman.com.

Kerrygold Butter and Cheese
To find out which supermarkets sell Kerrygold Irish butter and cheeses, contact the Irish Dairy Board, 825 Green Bay Road, Suite 200, Wilmette, IL 60091, phone 847-256-8289, or visit them online at www.kerrygold.com. Kerrygold is the international trademark of the Irish Dairy Board. To buy Kerrygold products, contact Traditional Irish Foods, 877-IRISHFOOD, or visit them online at www.foodireland.com.

Kinsale Brewing Company
This microbrewery is located in the scenic port town of Kinsale, in County Cork. For information on tours and tastings, visit them online at www.kinsalebrewing.com.

Knockeen Hills Irish Poteen
This poitín is made in County Waterford. For more information, visit them online at www.irish poteen.com.

Lakeshore Whole-Grain Mustard
Lakeshore Mustard, made in County Tipperary, is a delicious product available in some Irish import shops and from some online Irish food sites, such as Bewley Irish Imports. Phone 800-BEWLEY, or visit them online at www.bewley irishimports.com.

Locke's Distillery Museum
Established in 1757, Locke's is the last remaining example of a small pot distillery in Ireland. The distillery made pot still Irish malt whiskey for almost two hundred years. Locke's Distillery, in Kilbeggan, County Westmeath, is now open as a museum of industrial archaeology showing how whiskey was produced in times past. It's open for tours and tasting. For more information, visit them online at www.lockesdistillerymuseum.com.

Magners Irish Cider
In the United States, Bulmers Irish cider is marketed under the Magners brand. For more information, visit them online at: www.magners cider.com.

Meringues
Miss Meringue, based in San Marcos, California, is a delicious product available in most supermarkets. For more information, visit them online at www.missmeringue.com.

Murphy's Irish stout
This Cork-based brewery makes stout and Murphy's Irish Red, a red ale. For information, visit them online at www.murphysbeers.com.

Oatmeal
McCann's brand Irish oatmeal is available in most supermarkets. Both McCann's, Flahavans, and

Odlum's brands are available from Traditional Irish Foods, phone 877-IRISHFOOD, or visit them online at www.foodireland.com.

Old Bushmills Distillery

At the world's oldest licensed whiskey distillery, visitors can see the craftsmanship and skill involved in making an Irish single malt whiskey. During the tour, you will discover the secrets of the malted Irish barley, triple distillation, and aging processes. After the tour, you can relax in the 1608 Bar, have lunch in the Distillery Kitchen restaurant, and browse through the gift shop. The Old Bushmills Distillery is located in the village of Bushmills, in County Antrim. For information, email obd@whiskeytours.ie, or visit them online at www.whiskeytours.ie.

Old Jameson Distillery

When visitors enter the Old Jameson Distillery, they step back in time by almost two hundred years. The tour takes you through the story of John Jameson and his famous whiskey, guides you through a recreated scene of a working distillery, and then on to the warehouse and the bottling areas before culminating in the Jameson Bar for a whiskey tasting. A restaurant and gift shop are also on-site. In 1999, the distillery won the Dublin Tourism Supreme Award for best tourist experience. The Old Jameson Distillery is located on Bow Street, in the heart of Smithfield Village, in Dublin. For information, email ojd@whiskey tours.ie, or visit them online at www.whiskey tours.ie.

Old Midleton Distillery

At the Old Midleton Distillery, visitors can see the largest pot still in the world and the old waterwheel, which was manufactured in 1825 to provide power before the days of electricity. It's still turning today. Each tour culminates in the Jameson Bar at the Irish whiskey "tasting session," where visitors have the opportunity to become qualified "tasters" and receive a presentation diploma. Following the session, you can relax in the restaurant and browse through the gift and craft shops. The Old Midleton Distillery is located in Midleton, County Cork, a few miles east of Cork City. For information, email omd@whiskey tours.ie, or visit them online at www.whiskey tours.ie.

Poitín, *see also* Knockeen Hills Irish Poteen

In Ireland, you can visit the Bunratty Winery, located directly behind Bunratty Castle, in County Clare, to see how mead and poitín are made. To find out where you can buy them in the United States, contact Camelot Importing Co., phone 800-4-CAMELOT.

Shannon Heritage

Shannon Heritage is a wholly owned commercial subsidiary of Shannon Development Company and is one of the largest operators of heritage products in Europe. Starting out in 1962 with the medieval banquet at Bunratty Castle, it now presents a total of eight day-visitor experiences and four evening entertainments. For more information, visit them online at: www.shannonheritage.com.

Smoked Salmon

To order oak-smoked Irish salmon online, contact Traditional Irish Foods, 877-IRISHFOOD, or visit online at www.foodireland.com,

Tullamore Dew Heritage Centre

The Tullamore Dew Heritage Centre is housed in the original 1897 bonded warehouse in the busy town of Tullamore, in County Offaly. The exhibition tells the story of Tullamore Dew whiskey and the work that used to take place in the distillery, such as the malting, bottling, corking, cooperage, and maturing areas. The center, about an hour's drive from Dublin, also includes an area devoted to Irish Mist, a whiskey and honey-based spirit made there. Visitors can admire a community of 70,000 live bees that collect nectar for their queen. To contact, email tullamoredhc@eircom.net, or visit them online at www.tullamore-dew.org.

Whole-Wheat flour

Irish whole-wheat flour, such as Odlum's and Howard's brands, is available from Traditional Irish Foods, phone 877-IRISHFOOD, or visit them online at www.foodireland.com.

Williams-Sonoma

Founded in 1956, Williams-Sonoma is a specialty retailer of home furnishings and kitchenware. Its products are sold in retail stores, by catalog, and over the Internet. Visit them online at www.williams-sonoma.com.

TABLE of EQUIVALENTS

The exact equivalents in the following table has been rounded for convenience.

LIQUID/DRY MEASURES

U.S.	Metric
$1/4$ teaspoon	1.25 milliliters
$1/2$ teaspoon	2.5 milliliters
1 teaspoon	5 milliliters
1 tablespoon (3 teaspoons)	15 milliliters
1 fluid ounce (2 tablespoons)	30 milliliters
$1/4$ cup	60 milliliters
$1/3$ cup	80 milliliters
$1/2$ cup	120 milliliters
1 cup	240 milliliters
1 pint (2 cups)	480 milliliters
1 quart (4 cups; 32 ounces)	960 milliliters
1 gallon (4 quarts)	3.84 liters
1 ounce (by weight)	28 grams
1 pound	454 grams
2.2 pounds	1 kilogram

LENGTH

U.S.	Metric
$1/8$ inch	3 millimeters
$1/4$ inch	6 millimeters
$1/2$ inch	12 millimeters
1 inch	2.5 centimeters

OVEN TEMPERATURES

Fahrenheit	Celsius	Gas
250	120	$1/2$
275	140	1
300	150	2
325	160	3
350	180	4
375	190	5
400	200	6
425	220	7
450	230	8
475	240	9
500	260	10